COME FOLLOW ME

A Call to
Discipleship for the
Future Church.

Be a Loyal Learning Follower of Christ.

JAMES BARBER, D.MIN.

COME FOLLOW ME
A Call to Discipleship for the Future Church

ISBN: 978-1-940931-28-9
Library of Congress Control Number: 2025907696

Published by Timothy Publishing Services,
3409 W Gary St
Broken Arrow, OK
918-924-6246

Cover design by Felicia Cindyana, M.Div.
Cover photo purchased from AdobeStock.
Text Design/Layout: Lisa Simpson

Printed in the United States of America.
www.jbarberministries.org

**“Come Follow Jesus;
the Cost and Rewards
are Eternal!”**

— *Dr. James W Barber*

CONTENTS

DEDICATION

First, I acknowledge the significant power of the Holy Spirit in the event that occurred on October 17, 1982, which marked the beginning of my journey and calling into ministry. To Adeline (Addie), my precious wife, who encouraged me to the finish line and the completion of my Doctor of Ministry (D.Min.) Degree in 1997. She now presses me on to the completion of this text, my first published work.

To my pastors and mentors, Dr. Larry Lea, and Pastors Bob and the late Sue Farrar, at Church on the Rock (COTR), who called me out and sent me to seminary. They discipled me to become what they said I already had in me. Missions Director, Dr. David Shibley, who would later take me to India for the first time, is still active in my life and ministry.

My Oral Roberts University (ORU) colleagues and mentors: Dean Dr. Thomson (Thom) Mathew influenced my vocational transformation into chaplaincy, associate dean Dr. Cheryl Iverson taught me top notch administration, and theology professor Dr. Howard Ervin taught amazing depth of the biblical text regarding the Holy Spirit. These individuals are a few among many who have influenced me through the theological perspective described by Dr. Mathew as "Living Human Documents." I have also benefited from Dr. Ervin's continual encouragement to focus on discerning "What does the text say."

To all those who have helped me complete the research, edit and format this study for publication; ORU's editor Marlene Mankins, my D.Min. administrative secretary Celine Butler, and my dear church pastor Dr. Nancy Cook and parishioner and friend Ginger Cantrell, who completed numerous edits to my writing and gave me excellent feedback.

Finally, I could not have become this writer and started Barber Ministries Inc. (BMI), without the financial blessings of many people, especially that of Alan and Brenda Miller, who in 2005 helped me to launch this 501(c)3 ministry. It has been almost 30 years since I began the labor of documenting this research. I love the idea of putting things in print for people to see, read, and remember. I've heard it said that, "people will like what you say, but they never forget what you write." I feel that everything that I am worth and have become is engulfed in this treatise on discipleship. I pray that it blesses you on your journey as a disciple of Jesus Christ.

FOREWORD

When Jesus called The Twelve, He said to them, "Come follow me." Their response to this simple command changed not only their lives but also the course of world history. But what did that statement entail? It meant that they would be his apprentices; they would take upon themselves the yoke of his teaching, deeply committing themselves to learning everything they could; and be completely devoted to him.

Jesus' mandate to his followers was to "make disciples" – a critically vital component for the continuation of his movement. Yet, for many Christians the definition of a "disciple" can be confusing or even intimidating. What does it mean to be a "disciple" of Jesus? Can a woman be a disciple? How is a disciple "made?" And what are we expected to do?

Today, maybe more than ever, the body of believers needs to know the answers to these questions. If we are called to be disciples and to make disciples, it is imperative that we understand this important mandate that transcends generations and breaks the boundaries of culture, ethnicity, and gender.

In this book, Dr. James Barber simplifies the definition of discipleship and gives his readers a practical guide to becoming the disciples that Jesus calls us to be. He takes us through his own journey – as he shares a candid and transparent reflection of his life as a star Division 1 running back at Virginia Tech to the radical change that transpired as a result of his encounter with Christ and his later roles as hospice chaplain, pastor, and assistant professor at Oral Roberts University in Tulsa,

Oklahoma. His decades of experience in ministry and as an assistant professor are beautifully expressed in his presentation of effective and practical discipleship.

Dr. Barber reminds us that the fresh fire of following Jesus must be fueled by the power of the Holy Spirit. Each chapter shares practical, easy-to-read information about prayer, accountability, fellowship, and the importance of the Word of God. At the conclusion of each chapter, the reader has an opportunity to interact with the topic presented and an opportunity to interact with others about the material. This book combines years of practical experience with academic knowledge and presents a unique perspective concerning the concept of discipleship.

Nancy Cook, D. Min.
Senior Pastor, Tulsa Christian Center Ministries
Resident Adjunct Assistant Professor of Practical Theology
College of Theology and Ministry
Oral Roberts University

PREFACE

(My daughter, Christa Barber Moss, Esq.)

We live in a culture that emphasizes individualism, is strained by busyness, burdened by consumerism, and ravaged by political divisiveness. Our personal ambitions and professional goals, and even our kids' activities, drive our priorities; and I would be disingenuous not to admit that I have at times been more concerned with the social media worthiness of the aesthetic of my home, than sharing the convictions of my faith with others.

My father discipled me my entire life. I don't think I truly appreciated this until a few years ago, when I began serving at a new young church plant and witnessed to how I was saved at a young age and have been a Christian for as long as I can remember. I rarely doubted my faith or walked through periods of deconstruction. Though there are questions of faith I have often wrestled with, I remain deeply convicted to serve Jesus Christ as a result of my parent's spiritual direction in my life. I largely credit them for their steady devotion to their faith, both in how they lived it and how they encouraged me to reflect on the world as I watched them serve others.

I will never forget how frustrated I felt when I asked my father an important question about life or the Bible, or our faith, and my theology professor father would send me to a resource or a concordance, rather than telling me the answer directly. The older I grew, the more educated I became myself, the more he shared. Now, at nearly thirty-nine, and a lawyer, where my job is to question and research everything to death,

I am more aware than ever how the process of searching out an answer on your own, and seeking for revelation in the word, and praying, and wrestling with it by talking about it with other believers is crucial to not only your own spiritual growth but your ability to share those truths with others. Even more, with a family of my own to shepherd, I am challenged to facilitate and guide the development of their faith.

My father has been studying and researching discipleship for longer than I have been alive, nearly 40 years of his life. He has taught hundreds of students and ministered all across the world. I have seen him make sacrifices in total devotion to the calling in his life to take the gospel to the ends of the earth and share with everyone he meets that the most important thing they could ever do is find relationship with Jesus.

Everyone is being discipled; the question is by whom? The culture we live in today is highly demanding of our time, and primarily focused on all that we can accomplish for ourselves. There is little time for prioritizing what is most important about our faith.

Christa Barber Moss, Esq.
Kansas City, KS
2025

INTRODUCTION

THE COST OF BECOMING A DISCIPLE

The biblical concept of discipleship denotes a spiritual commitment to the model that God expects from all believers.

The pastor's message at the church on the Sunday that I decided to attend because of the insistence of my then girlfriend, Miriam, was based on the text in Matthew 18:19. The scripture discusses the importance of agreement in one's pursuit for a common purpose in God's will.

> *Again I say to you, if two of you agree on earth about anything they ask, it will be done for them by my Father in heaven. (Matt. 18:19)*

I originally made a reference to my relationship with my girlfriend Miriam to this text, but the pastor's sermon on agreement struck a chord when I audibly heard the voice of the Holy Spirit say, *"James, you need to agree with me."* That day, October 17, 1982, became my first 180-degree turning point, with the Spirit leading me to align with God's will instead of following my own desires. For the first time in my existence, I walked the aisle and made Jesus Christ Lord of my life.

I felt like I had been a failure due to the setbacks in my life: not becoming a professional football player, being terminated from my college football coaching position, and the failure of my first marriage. On that day I felt the weight of all I had gone through lift as the Holy Spirit began guiding me to acknowledge my salvation and embrace being an overcomer through God's power. Until then, I had seen only failure and loss without any understanding of the true cost that came that day when I made Jesus Christ Lord.

In retrospect, I have to start with the fact that I was raised in a Presbyterian church environment, where everything was a suggestion, and not a biblical requirement. I do not recall hearing that my life should be submitted or related to Jesus, or to become an example of the biblical understanding of Jesus Christ's relationship to his disciples. The religious tradition I grew up with did not emphasize a relationship with the Holy Spirit or require changes to my lifestyle, tithing, prayer, or studying God's Word.

At 30 years of age, I was suddenly asked by God to abandon everything I knew and valued. In the self-indulgent era of the 70s and 80s, I led a carefree life that included smoking pot in college and experiencing marital issues that ended in divorce from Geraldine, mother of twin NFL legends, Tiki and Ronde Barber. After my divorce and losing my coaching job at Virginia Tech, I worked in restaurant management and as a waiter. This time was dominated by sex, drugs, and rock 'n' roll, and I was heavily involved.

Fast forward to after my conversion in 1982. I eventually became a member and volunteer in the Adult Singles Ministry at Church On The Rock (COTR) in Rockwall, Texas. The work at COTR encompassed four main discipleship practices commonly seen in the Charismatic movement: prayer to Father God, Biblical study of his word, fellowship with believers, and evangelism to a world that is in desperate need of Jesus Christ. This transformation can only be described by me as a "Jump Culture" phenomenon.

The term "Jump Culture" was coined while I attended Oral Roberts University (ORU) pursuing two degrees in theology, Master of Divinity (M.Div.) and Doctor of Ministry (D.Min.). The "Jump Culture" progression involves the change that occurs when an individual continues to work out their salvation as the Apostle Paul encourages the believers at Philippi:

> *Therefore, my beloved, as you have always obeyed, so now, not only as in my presence but much more in my absence, work out your own salvation with fear and trembling, for it is God who works in you, both to will and to work for his good pleasure. (Phil. 2:12–13)*

This process describes Dr. Larry Lea, pastor of COTR, becoming a Spirit-filled believer after his Holy Spirit encounter in the 70s. His transition from his Baptist background to becoming a charismatic believer was a "Jump Culture" event adopting a new approach seen nationwide during the Charismatic Movement of the 70s and 80s.

His transformation affected me in such a way that I can only call what I encountered a prayer revival with Dr. Lea and his ministry at COTR, written about in his book, "Could You Not Tarry One Hour."[1]

His sacrifice for those early morning prayer vigils captivated the city and influenced people all over the globe. Renowned

---

[1] Larry Lea, *Could You Not Tarry: Learning the Joy of Prayer* (Altamonte Springs, FL Creation House, 1987).

pastors like Paul Yonggi Cho, (Yoido Full Gospel Church, Seoul, South Korea) and Oral Granville Roberts (Oral Roberts University, Tulsa, OK.) were inspired. Other charismatic ministers also based their churches on early Christian Holy Spirit encounters like those mentioned in the book of Acts, and the concept of using cell groups, which Dr. Lea called the 20/20 vision from Acts 20:20.

> *[H]ow I did not shrink from declaring to you anything that was profitable and teaching you in public and from house to house, testifying both to Jews and to Greeks of repentance toward God and of faith in our Lord Jesus Christ. (Acts 20:20–21)*

This passage of scripture became the outline for what happens in cell groups. This was in the church, and it was from house to house. I have called this the "The Big Four" of Prayer, Word, Fellowship, and Evangelism.

> *And they devoted themselves to the apostles' teaching and the fellowship, to the breaking of bread and the prayers. And awe came upon every soul, and many wonders and signs were being done through the apostles. And all who believed were together and had all things in common. And they were selling their possessions and belongings and distributing the proceeds to all, as any had need. (Acts 2:42–45)*

Dr. Lea believed these groups could operate anywhere: in churches, in homes, in communities, online and worldwide. As a result of this phenomenon, I became a cell group leader in the Adult Singles Ministry at COTR, connecting people with similar diverse interests.

The singles ministry included retirees, professionals, and single adults from various backgrounds—never married, people seeking marriage partners, or divorced individuals seeking to reconnect their lives. It was in this group I would meet my future wife, Adeline, from India, who was attending Christ for the Nations Institute (CFNI). Prior to our relationship I believed that my undertaking for ministry would be like the Apostle Paul, not to be married, but of course, I knew that my desire was not to be *unmarried* like the Apostle.

I met Adeline (Addie) in a cell group I led for the single adults' ministry at COTR. One evening in the group meeting, I talked about attending a mission school set up by ORU and a Bible college to evangelize individuals in northern India. The school was created to win souls and train believers for evangelism. During that cell group meeting, I heard her say, "He will never survive it in India." When I asked who said that, I recognized that it was Adeline. I asked her why she would say that, and she responded that I wouldn't like India because of the people, the customs, and you could not get your Cokes, chips and cookies.

During this period, I became acquainted with Adeline, an Indian nurse visiting with extensive knowledge of the villages and customs of India. We subsequently married in December 1985. We were highly involved in lay ministry as the congregation of COTR grew, and the need for ministers increased to meet the growth when I was asked to join the staff in Rockwall in 1986.

In the fall of 1986, I took distance education classes at Oral Roberts University through the church. Later that year, we decided I should complete my education more quickly. Thus, in the fall of 1988, we chose to move to Tulsa, Oklahoma and attend ORU full-time, following Dr. Lea's challenge to study either in India or at ORU.

During these early years of my lay ministry the then Singles Pastors Bob and Sue Farrar had formed teaching groups around The Navigator Series *Design for Discipleship*, with the main purpose of strengthening our lives as believers. For most of us, the result was part of the Fire that was started by Dr. Lea in Rockwall. The Adult Singles Ministry grew to over 200 men and women. For me it was a renewed hope for the future, and deeper relationships with our fellow brothers and sisters, which provided a stronger relationship with God.

The cell group ministry helped me understand what it meant to be a true minister and a disciple: serving, submitting to authority, praying, and studying the word. The leaders mentored us, showing what it meant to follow Christ and lead in a pastoral role. This culture of prayer, study, and fellowship was unlike anything I'd experienced before, either in my small Presbyterian church in Charlotte or as a football coach at Virginia Tech.

While I began my role at COTR by leading cell groups, I became the lead staff pastor for the Adults Singles Ministry. In 1988, while serving as a staff pastor in COTR, Dr. Lea approached me and discussed the possibility of traveling to India to establish a ministry and educational programs at the bible school that he had helped establish. We were given the option to go to India as missionaries and complete the M.Div. degree under Dr. P. J. Titus, attending the COTR Bible School in Vishakhapatnam in Andra Predesh, India, or attending Oral Roberts University full-time for the M.Div. Degree.

Dr. Titus and his wife Mary left Dallas, TX, to serve in Visakhapatnam, to start a Bible school to train young men and women to help establish God's Kingdom in Northern India. Pastor Lea suggested I go to India to see if I felt the calling, otherwise, I should attend ORU. I planned to get my M.Div. degree while working in India, excited about mission work and education.

However, India presented unexpected challenges that deepened my understanding of faith and my relationship with God. On the first night of a crusade in Hyderabad, two men brought their friend, apparently cursed by a witch and demon-possessed, and asked me to cast out the demon. His eyes were red, his face contorted, and he looked at me with rage. This was my first encounter with a demon in my 30 years of life and faith.

I felt an inclination to follow the directive in the text and lay hands on him to pray. However, I was guided by the Holy Spirit who reminded me, *"Do not be hasty in the laying on of hands, nor take part in the sins of others; keep yourself pure," (1 Tim. 5:22).* Consequently, I directed them to the front of the church stage where several pastors gathered around him. They laid hands on him and cast out the demon as he convulsed on the ground in the crusade stadium. This experience was unlike anything I had ever witnessed, and I was totally unprepared for such an event.

Upon returning, I shared this encounter with the search team and later with Dr. Lea, expressing my thoughts: "I think I need to attend the ORU seminary." I spent the next nine years at Oral Roberts University, obtaining my M.Div. and D.Min. degrees. Dr. Lea recommended that some of my educational expenses could be subsidized by COTR, provided I worked as an Assistant Pastor at the Church on the Rock in Tulsa. in a role similar to my role in Rockwall.

The education and experiences I gained at ORU were irreplaceable. The professors, along with my educational and ministry colleagues, significantly contributed to my preparation for serving as a teacher and minister in the kingdom of God. Although the school in India would have allowed me to continue a route of missions, I ultimately decided to pursue higher education at Oral Roberts University, believing that a degreed education was essential for success. I aimed to complete two degrees, the M.Div. Degree and the D.Min. Degree, with the intention of returning to Rockwall, TX, to further the mission and vision of the church and teach in the Bible School in India.

Even after starting cell group ministry at COTR, I was uncertain about continuing on the path of full-time ministry until a prophetic minister, Dick Mills, addressed me among a group at the altar. He was inviting those interested in future teaching or ministry involvement. Dr. Larry Lea had also prophesied that I would be involved in ministry, but I was reluctant. Prophet Mills called me out and the prophecy went something like this:

"Son, come up here. You have a honey bucket of anointing flowing all over you, and you are called to go to the nations. You will go around the world and will lead many people to Christ, and you will operate in every gift and have favor from God. By the way, don't worry; you will not have to call them; they will call you."

At this point, I recognized a clear calling for ministry in my life and understood that involvement required more than simply attending a church which eventually led as we know to attending Oral Roberts University full-time.

When I began seminary at ORU in 1988, one of my favorite professors, Dr. Charles Snow, shared what has become a mantra for me that I have remembered and still use till this day. He said, "A disciple is a loyal, learning, follower of Jesus Christ." I never forgot this phrase. I am even more appreciative of what it means to be a living model as a disciple following Christ in four specific processes of prayer, word, fellowship and evangelism

As a matter of mechanics, we see that Jesus operated in the same four specific areas mentioned above regardless of ethnicity or culture, namely, discipleship does not discriminate or separate. We cannot help but see these four things; Prayer and Intercession to Father God *(proseuche)*; The Written and Uttered Word of God *(Didache, Rhema)*; The Application of True Fellowship *(koinonia)*; and Caring Cultural Evangelism to a world that is in desperate need of a relationship with Jesus Christ *(Euaggelizo).*

Dr. Snow explained that being a disciple involves making more disciples, continuously echoing the "Follow Me" concept mentioned 20 times in the Gospels, especially by Jesus when he said, "Come Follow Me." This discipleship was observed in the teachings and practices of Old Testament Patriarchs, Prophets, Jesus Christ, Apostle Paul, and The Twelve. They taught both men and women to be disciples, just as Jesus did.

When I began teaching discipleship in the church, a woman approached me asking, "What about the women?" She pointed out that women followed Jesus and heard his teachings. The text referred to both men and women, including those women who were not often mentioned from the pulpit. There were many, like the woman who touched the hem of Jesus' garment in Matthew 9:20. I guarantee you she started to follow him. How about the woman at the well (John 4:7)? I believe she became so enthralled that she followed Jesus too. Then there is Mary, sitting at his feet, wiping with her tears and her hair she kissed his feet and poured ointment on him (John 11:2). I assert that discipleship is not exclusive to men, a position I detail in Chapter 8.

My thesis, completed in 1997, was based on the four principles of discipleship related to men. Initially, the goal was to teach discipleship to the entire church because the principles of discipleship are essential for the whole congregation, who are all called to be disciples. However, at the direction of the Director of the D.Min. Program, my thesis needed to be significantly limited and focused only on men in small groups in the local Church. When I approached the Director of the D.Min. Program, Dr. Thomson Mathew, he recommended I narrow the scope to focus on groups. Because my wife and I were pastors of the singles fellowship at the church, I decided to do the singles leaders, men and women as a group. When Dr. Mathew instructed me to narrow it down even further, I began to recruit men in small groups to be disciples.

I completed my thesis in 1997 with the title "Discipling Men in Small Groups in the Local Church." I began to associate with the Promise Keepers Movement and received permission to use their material and as a result have successfully continued to base my lessons on the seven principles taught by Promise Keepers. As I persisted in my study and research, I continued to see the same four overarching principles of Prayer, Word, Fellowship, and Evangelism, naming them "The Big Four."

Prayer serves as a foundation for an individual's communication with God. According to the teachings of Jesus, prayer was integral, as he regularly sought opportunities to engage in this form of dialogue with the Father. Dr. Larry Lea's work, "Could You Not Tarry One Hour," emphasizes that prayer is an essential practice for all believers. Without engaging in prayer and fostering agreement with God and others, it is unlikely that individuals will experience meaningful responses or spiritual outcomes.

The second point concerns the Word of God. The Word in context provides the deeper insights that are essential for successful elements related to the principles of discipleship. Biblical teaching and guidance from knowledgeable teachers help deepen our comprehension beyond our own assumptions. After Prayer, God's word provides another connection to the Father God. Prayers related to and based on the biblical text will provide a deeper relationship with those who pray together.

Fellowship is the third concept, where prayer and the Word of God meet. Churches have through history emphasized activities like Sunday school fellowship, church socials, and the Sunday morning and evening services. The latest phenomenon is different small home group meetings throughout the week.

True discipleship means that church gathering, eating, teaching, and sharing are just as Jesus did with his followers,

> *And as Jesus reclined at table in the house, behold, many tax collectors and sinners came and were reclining with Jesus and his disciples. (Matthew 9:10)*

Acts 2:42 highlights the church's purpose, calling for *koinonia* (Greek for fellowship), or face-to-face connection as seen with Jesus with for all believers, beyond just listening to sermons.

> *And they devoted themselves to the apostles' teaching and the fellowship, to the breaking of bread and the prayers. And awe came upon every soul, and many wonders and signs were being done through the apostles. And all who believed were together and had all things in common. And they were selling their possessions and belongings and distributing the proceeds to all, as any had need. And day by day, attending the temple together and breaking bread in their homes, they received their food with glad and generous hearts, praising God and having favor with all the people. And the Lord added to their number day by day those who were being saved. (Acts 2:42-47)*

Evangelism is the fourth principal, as found in the last sentence in the text above, which is outreach or witness. A crucial element of evangelism is mobility, as the concept meets people where they are living and visiting. Acts chapter 2, says that as a result, those who come in share all things in common.

We see here there was no lack, or need, or purposes that the church could or should not meet in the common sense with people who believe like each other. These "Big Four" principles involve more than helping others to get saved; it also conveys *Sozo* i.e., salvation, healing, and deliverance.

Disciples are called to reach out to a world that is in desperate need of Jesus Christ. True discipleship has prayer, word, fellowship and evangelism as the four aspects that will be perused in this study. In Matthew 28, Jesus' last commandment to His disciples was to "GO" make disciples. The text is clear,

> *Go therefore and make disciples of all nations, baptizing them in the name of the Father and of the Son and of the Holy Spirit, teaching them to observe all that I have commanded you. And behold, I am with you always, to the end of the age. (Matt. 28:19–20)*

For the past 30 years, I have valued the experiences of culture from world travels making disciples in all nations. ORU has a student population at the time of this writing representing over 140 nations. The majority of my teaching and travels were the result of my students inviting me to their countries.

The disciples were tasked with encouraging individuals to make decisions in alignment with the teachings of Jesus Christ. Various approaches are explored to teach discipleship, with an emphasis on methods that reflect the principles attributed to Jesus Christ. Religious leaders often concentrate on these teaching strategies. These principles have longstanding roots and appear throughout historical and biblical records.

The Baptism of the Holy Spirit is essential to understand what God expects from Jesus Christ's followers; we will examine these principles found in the Gospels and the book of Acts. These accounts will bring us into a new focus of the future Church, starting with this baptism of fire in the upper room. The Holy Spirit would bring to the disciples' remembrance the principles taught by Jesus as crucial for modern church beliefs and the role of the Holy Spirit in believers' lives.

> *When the day of Pentecost arrived, they were all together in one place. And suddenly there came from heaven a sound like a mighty rushing wind, and it filled the entire house where they were sitting. And divided tongues as of fire appeared to them and rested on each one of them. And they were all filled with the Holy Spirit and began to speak in other tongues as the Spirit gave them utterance. (Acts 2:1–4)*

This initial Spirit infilling marked a significant moment for the church. The baptism of the Holy Spirit at this juncture is viewed by some as a primary means for the church's progress in the world. As more individuals joined after this beginning, the movement grew rapidly. The Holy Spirit is referenced as an empowering force on all that were in the upper room.

> *And they devoted themselves to the apostles' teaching and the fellowship, to the breaking of bread and the prayers. And awe came upon every soul, and many wonders and signs were being done through the apostles. And all who believed were together and had all things in common. And they were selling their possessions and belongings and distributing the proceeds to all, as any had need. And day by day, attending the temple together and breaking bread in their homes, they received their food with glad and generous hearts, praising God and having favor with all the people. And the Lord*

added to their number day by day those who were being saved. (Acts 2:42-47)

Today, Spirit-filled disciples of Jesus Christ follow Him with the same dedication and modesty, developing characteristics that resemble his characteristics. As these individuals grow in their understanding, they become involved in related ministries, shaping their behavior based on the example provided by Jesus. This approach has led to the expansion of discipleship with the Holy Spirit contributing to its growth and the church continuing to expand. This method has been effective globally, impacting many countries. The principles that were central to Jesus' teachings are causing those fellowships implementing them to experience significant growth.

Discipleship transforms individuals to become more like Jesus Christ, turning learners into leaders, mentors, and teachers. This transformation adds to the Church through the Holy Spirit's influence. The Great Commission in Matthew (Matt 28:18-20) instructs the Church to make disciples of all nations. The methodology of the "Big Four" of Prayer, Word, Fellowship and Evangelism can be applied anywhere. Discipleship is defined as a group of believers committed to Jesus Christ, aiming to impact themselves and their generation through "The Big Four."

In today's churches, the call is for believers to be loyal, learning followers of Christ who generate in others the belief that they must continue to be strategic goal-setters, and essential providers of discipleship for the church. This happened for me in the midst of the revival in Rockwall at COTR with its many fundamentals, especially the teaching related to discipleship, church growth, the multiplication process in the small group ministry, the daily early morning prayer ministry, and the city-wide evangelism. I felt a definite change and was compelled to do more than be a passive believer.

My education at ORU produced by far some of the best instructions and infusions into my life. The professors and my educational and ministry colleagues have aided in my preparation for working as a teacher and a minister in the kingdom of God. As I look back on that time, I am aware that many friends, cell group leaders, pastors and professors were all divine appointments.

When I experienced the significant life change in 1982, I recalled individuals who were instrumental in shaping the pivotal moments that led to my transformation. Craig Valentine, a former football teammate, found faith during the Jesus Movement that started in the late 60s. He attended a Jesus Movement meeting at Virginia Tech, similar to others happening nationwide, and embraced it fully.

He came to me one day pleading, "JB, you have got to go with me to this meeting."

"What was that?" I asked.

"Man, I just got saved, and you need to come and go with me."

"No, Craig, I know the Jesus thing, and I don't need it here. Besides, I grew up with that Jesus stuff in Baptist vacation Bible school and Presbyterian Boy Scouts!"

Years later, at a Virginia Tech Football reunion, Craig was there also. He looked at me and immediately said, "JB, you got it, didn't you?"

I said, "Man, ever since I got saved, and received the Holy Spirit's infilling, you were one of the first persons I thought about after my 1982 conversion." The Holy Spirit orchestrated this contribution from people like Craig Valentine, confirming that God was wanting to do this in the 70s. The Holy Spirit's influence in meeting our needs also applies to the means by which we will receive that assistance. It could be people, places or circumstances that we see ensuring that we eventually achieve the goals that have been set for us to achieve by God's plan.

During my years at Virginia Tech, there was this annoying fellow named William Magnuson who constantly handed out those "Chick Tracks," it seemed especially to me. My roommate during this period was Bruce Arians, a supportive Catholic, who also prayed for and encouraged me. Bruce and I played football at Virginia Tech from 1970-1974, and then coached there from 1975-1977. Bruce continued a successful career as a head coach in the National Football League (NFL) with the Arizona Cardinals from 2013–2017, and the Tampa Bay Buccaneers from 2019-2021.

Following one's salvation, discipleship serves as the pathway to that success, deepening our relationship with God and aiding others in finding Him. This is particularly important as you learn to be a loyal follower of Christ, as Jesus taught, by practicing prayer, studying the Word of God, fellowship, and evangelism. Through these practices, I am confident that Father God, Jesus Christ and the Holy Spirit would be well pleased.

My prayer is that you will become a true disciple of the master Jesus Christ and more so a loyal, learning, follower and living human document of the discipleship principles that Jesus taught. The result will enable you to become deeply involved in relationships with your colleagues, neighbors, friends, and a loving outreach to the world around you that is in desperate need of a relationship with Jesus Christ.

Dr. James W. Barber

CHAPTER 1

A DISCIPLE AND JESUS CHRIST

A DISCIPLE IS COMMITTED TO HONORING JESUS CHRIST THROUGH WORSHIP, PRAYER, AND OBEDIENCE TO GOD'S WORD THROUGH THE POWER OF THE HOLY SPIRIT

In 1982, just weeks before my 30th birthday, my mother called one evening as I sat in my living room in Dallas, TX. I loved this city; its big-ness, its busy-ness, the TV show "Dallas," and the Dallas Cowboys. I had just been laid off from my job as a restaurant manager. I do not know how Mom heard that I had been terminated, but she heard about it, probably from my sister Brenda, with whom I talked frequently. The conversation went like this:

> *"Son, I heard that you lost your job. You know you can always come home. I've been praying for you, and I am done chasing you all over the country, so I went to see the pastor at our church. We just got together and prayed for you, and he*

directed that they pray what the text said. So, son, we have turned your life over to Satan for the destruction of your flesh. You are living outside of the will of God, so we prayed that He (God) will deliver you and change your life."

She referenced a passage from 1 Corinthians 5:5 "*...you are to deliver this man to Satan for the destruction of the flesh, so that his spirit may be saved on the day of the Lord.*" She stressed that this was God's Word, meant to save me from my chosen path. My mother's words haunted me because I barely understood scripture.

During my tenure as an assistant manager at the restaurant, I developed a relationship with one of the hostesses, named Miriam. We discussed our future together, including the possibility of marriage. However, since she was in the process of obtaining a divorce, our relationship was put on hold. She suggested I attend church with her. I agreed to go on Sunday, October 17, 1982.

Miriam emphasized that a relationship with Jesus was key to understanding the biblical text and even my mother's words, even though I grew up in a Presbyterian church that rarely, in my understanding, ever focused much on heaven or hell.

On that Sunday in October, the minister in the charismatic church that I attended with Miriam was sharing from the Gospel of Matthew. As a young man, I could quote you the order of the books in order, from Genesis to Revelation, but I had never really read the Bible. But the pastor at Miriam's church quoted Matthew 18: 19-20:

Again, I say to you, if two of you agree on earth about anything they ask, it will be done for them by my Father in heaven. For where two or three are gathered in my name, there am I among them.

The words prompted me to think that I could ask God for just what I wanted, and he would give it to me. For Miriam and I to be together, and eventually marry. Suddenly, for the first time in my life, in my right ear, I heard an internal but very audible voice. *"James, you need to agree with me."*

I had never had this experience with who I now know to be Jesus Christ. It was a voice that literally invaded my soul. The minister said as if he were looking directly at me, "If you hear God speaking to you right now, you need to come forward!" I was taken aback. I had heard ministers say that before, but now I heard a palpable voice from God. I responded to the altar call in what I can only describe as one of many *180-degree turning points* in my life.

For the first time, I really gave my life to Jesus that day. I decided it was time to up my game and respond to what had happened at church that day. I came home, and I began to read my Bible, listen to Christian radio and watch Christian television.

It was a continuation of the morning service and the result of my mother's prayer when a TV minister called out from his message and said, "You are a businessman under conviction because you need more than salvation; you need the baptism of the Holy Spirit!"

I immediately knew he was talking to and about me. At his invitation, I got on my knees and confessed Jesus as my Lord and Savior, and that I needed the baptism of the Holy Spirit. The TV minister then instructed,

> *"If that is you, I am now asking you to invite the Holy Spirit Baptism into your life with the evidence of 'Speaking in Tongues.'"*

He exhorted the listeners after we had prayed not to speak in English but to utter the first words that would come out of my mouth. To me, what I uttered sounded like baby talk, and then he encouraged the listeners to keep going, which I did.

At that moment, I heard Satan say, "That is not of God!" The minister responded as if he heard the devil. "Don't you listen to the Devil say, 'That this not of God!'" I knew inside that this was the Spirit speaking, and I began to speak more fluently, knowing inside I was baptized in the Spirit. After this experience, I began to practice and look for more of this in the Word of God and study more about the gifts of the Holy Spirit.

Where was this teaching being taught, and who believed and practiced this? Being raised in a Presbyterian environment I was not aware, except in a joking sense, of the Pentecostal charismatic church. Speaking in tongues was taught in Presbyterian and Baptist churches to be a gift that was not for today. However, growing up we had neighbors who spoke in tongues. It never bothered us, but it never captivated and encouraged us to participate.

As I began to read the Bible after my conversion in the 80s with this new Holy Spirit anointing, I was catapulted into a whole new existence I had never known for thirty years. This began the Holy Spirit search, with teaching from sources like radio, television, Christian bookstores and assistance from my newly Spirit-filled sister Brenda, who had started attending a charismatic church in her hometown. Practically all of our conversations were about my new experience with this third person of the Godhead, the Holy Spirit. I started attending several churches. People invited me to their charismatic or Pentecostal church.

The one thing I found out is that the central theme of the Pentecostal/Charismatic movement was Jesus Christ and the Holy Spirit. Everyone worshipped differently, but I found the experience enlightening and exciting. This led me to Church On The Rock in Rockwall, Texas, guided by Dr. Larry Lea, where I began my spiritual journey. COTR, a charismatic church, became my home with its classes, cell groups, and Spirit-filled teachings. It was there that I learned to pray.

How I Began to Pray

I was working part-time at the 700 Club after being terminated from my job as a restaurant manager. I also found an additional job as a waiter and manager in training at another restaurant when I met my dear friend Linda Miller and her husband Howard. Linda was an older waitress at this restaurant and encouraged me,

"You've got to come to my church; it is my FAMILY! Church on The Rock!"

It was as if she said it in all caps. I had seen the signs on the highway that Linda had referenced: "FAMILY! CHURCH ON THE ROCK." That word stuck in my mind– "Family"-- so, when Linda mentioned it, I decided I would visit. On the day that I visited the church, I met one of the men who would become instrumental in my decision to attend ORU, and who remains a mentor to this day, Missions Pastor, Dr. David Shibley. He was sharing about missions and the ministry of COTR. I was so impressed that evening with Shibley's teaching and preaching style, plus the fact that he believed in missions, that I decided I wanted to be a member of this church, COTR.

In 1988, Dr. Shibley would offer me the opportunity to go on what would be my first mission trip and my first visit to India, the birthplace and former home of my wife, Adeline. He has continued to be a colleague that I turn to for advice related to international ministry.

I had been at COTR for about a year when Dr. Lea shared in a Wednesday night service that we were no longer going to have the traditional Wednesday night service as we had historically known it. He instructed everyone to find a place, stand, kneel, or sit, however they chose to pray. He instructed everyone to begin to pray in the Spirit for one minute if they could.

I only realized how difficult a task this would be when, after about 10 or 15 seconds, there was a sudden lull in the church. Dr. Lea encouraged us to keep going. After one minute, he stopped us and said, "We all have the desire to pray, but we don't have the discipline that leads to the delight of prayer." He introduced what I call the three mantras of prayer: *Desire, Discipline, and Delight.*

This 3-word mantra began a series of teachings on the Lord's Prayer. From that moment, Dr. Lea began to teach the concept of prayer based on these three mantras. He taught that evening,

> *"We all have a desire to pray, but it requires discipline to pray as Jesus did, and after a period, you begin to experience the delight that comes from praying to the Father. What you are about to see is that model."*

This first lesson is related to *how* I began to pray. I do not want you to see it as a formula; I want you to see it as Jesus taught it.

I started reciting the Lord's Prayer at a young age. No one had ever taught us about its true meaning, other than the fact that it was a rote prayer for most people. My wife was raised as a Catholic believer, and she prayed the Lord's Prayer with her rosaries and never thought about its meaning. People everywhere have prayed the Lord's Prayer at the beginning or the end of a meeting, a speech, a lecture, or a church service.

In Luke 11:1-2, Jesus' disciples asked Him, "*Lord, teach us to pray just as John taught his disciples.*" Jesus then teaches them to pray, which we refer to today as the Lord's Prayer; "*When you pray. . .*" and we know the rest. When I was in seminary, Dr. Brad Young called it the Disciple's Prayer, which is why it is such an important part of discipleship. The first lesson we need to learn is how to pray using the Lord's Prayer as an outline.

In my experience as a believer, I had not prayed the way Dr. Lea had taught us to pray; to simply use the Lord's Prayer as the format or an outline to follow. In his book "Could You Not Tarry One Hour," Dr. Lea describes a conversation that he had with Dr. Cho and Dr. Criswell of First Baptist in Dallas, Texas. Dr. Criswell jokingly confided:

> *"Cho, when I pray for 15 minutes, I feel as if I've worn God out and worn myself out, too. How can you pray as you pray? How do you do it? How do you pray? Dr. Lea said, 'I'm so glad Cho did not give Criswell a traditional Pentecostal answer such as, I speak in tongues, and you don't.' Instead, Cho smiled graciously and said, 'Every morning, I get on a 'running track' in the Spirit, and I circle that track. I know that when I'm one-fifth of the way through, two-fifths, four-fifths, and then, finally, I know when I'm done. Then, if I have time, I run it again and again, just as a runner would circle a track.'"*[2]

A Club is all You Need

Rockwall represented one of several significant *180-degree turning points* transitions I experienced. I had been in the stupor of drugs, sex, and waywardness of life since my college days at Virginia Tech from 1970-1974.

One day, following my conversion experience in 1982, I heard the director of the 700 Club in Dallas, TX, John Kendall, speaking of the need for phone counselors for the program. I immediately got in my car and went to the 700 Club. I made no

---

[2] Larry Lea, 180.

connections between the fact that this was a recorded program and not a live broadcast.

When I met John, he informed me that the program he recorded was several months old. I immediately knew I wanted to know this man. I began to work at the 700 Club for a few hours a week, and then they offered me a paid position as a part-time counselor. I started calling the 700 Club, *"The Club"* because I was particularly drawn to the daily devotions which were a part of John's daily teaching method. One day, he invited me to his house, where I met his wife, Marsha. This was a unique family; they immediately adopted me and taught me, among other things, how to read the Word of God, how to pray, and how to be forgiven, which I really needed.

One day, John's assistant Mark Meinshine asked me, *"James, did you hear from God today?"*

I replied, *"Was I supposed to? Was this Hear from God Day?"*

Mark laughed and then handed me a Strong's Concordance. He suggested that I use it when I have daily devotional time, or when I read the word, prayed, or wanted to check something that I heard from the Holy Spirit. When I read or heard words that I didn't understand, I could look them up in the Strong's Concordance.

I replied, *"I have one of those in the back of my Bible."*

Mark laughed again. "*That's not a Concordance; that's just a Bible dictionary. This concordance has every word in the Bible; you will need this in the years to come.*"

As I look back, these divine appointments have led me to realize how much God orchestrates and works in our lives and sends people to disciple us. He even leads us to a place that is inclusive, where we learn, mature and get what we need from God. For me, that was "The Club."

John, Marsha and Mark served as my first dedicated discipleship leaders. They gave me so much advice and direction that I truly value them to this day. Right before John Kendall passed away, I met with him and his wife Marsha for the last time before he passed into eternity.

John and Marsha shared how proud they were of me and what I had become from the first days of being at "The Club;" how I had become a minister of the gospel, a professor and Director of the Doctor of Ministry Program at one of the major Association of Theological Schools (ATS) in the country. After over 30 years of attending and teaching, I can never discount the 700 Club's contributions to my development with those first little starts, steps and advancements which led to much growth. After my seminary education, I realized how much God's direction and those divine appointments have helped to guide and fulfill God's will in my life.

After each chapter in this workbook, there will be a lesson to solidify each individual's growth and development as a disciple. This lesson will focus on Prayer. These end-of-chapter lessons can also be used in small groups to help further the vocational identity on how to successfully become a loyal learning follower of Jesus Christ.

Lesson for Chapter 1

A Disciple and Jesus Christ

A DISCIPLE IS COMMITTED TO HONORING JESUS CHRIST THROUGH WORSHIP, PRAYER, AND OBEDIENCE TO GOD'S WORD THROUGH THE POWER OF THE HOLY SPIRIT[3]

CORE ISSUE:

Intimacy with Jesus will require obedience, but it will also require getting instructions and directions on how to obey. Prayer is the avenue that not only brings you intimacy with God, but also direction from God.

KEY PASSAGE:

Whom have I in heaven but you? And there is nothing on earth that I desire besides you. (Ps. 73:25)

[3] All lessons adapted and used by permission from: John Trent, ed. *Go the Distance.* Promise Keepers-(Focus on the Family, 1996); & Horner, Bob, Ron Ralston, & David Sundae. *Promise Builders: Applying the Seven Promises.* (Promise Keepers. Focus on the Family, 1996); & Al Janssen, & Larry K. Weeden, ed. *Seven Promises of a Promise Keeper:* (Promise Keepers. Focus on the Family, 1994), All rights reserved-ed. International copyright secured. Used by permission.

WARM-UP DISCUSSION:

For some, "risky" is losing your job at age 45, walking to a corner market in the inner city, giving a report before your peers, or being admitted to the hospital. For others, just telling their friends how bad their day was is scary enough. What is the riskiest thing you can remember doing? Why did you do it?

BACKGROUND:

After seeing Jesus feed over 5,000 men and women with a kid's sack lunch and receiving a prayer lesson on how to have a conversation with the Father God, Peter must have emerged with a great deal of confidence in his Lord's ability to provide in every imaginable situation. Within a few hours, however, Jesus asked Peter to do something he had never done before – in fact, something so risky that Peter would never have tried it, unless the Lord Himself directed him to it.

LET'S READ THE WORD:

Luke 9:14–16; 11:1-4; Matt. 6:13; 14:28-33

For there were about five thousand men. And he said to his disciples, "Have them sit down in groups of about fifty each." And they did so and had them all sit down. And taking the five loaves and the two fish, he looked up to heaven and said a blessing over them. Then he broke the loaves and gave them to the disciples to set before the crowd. And they all ate and were satisfied. And what was left over was picked up, twelve baskets of broken pieces. (Luke 9:14–16 ESV)

Now Jesus was praying in a certain place, and when he finished, one of his disciples said to him, "Lord, teach us to pray, as John taught his disciples." And he said to them, "When you pray, say: "Father, hallowed be your name. Your kingdom come. Give us each day our daily bread, and forgive us our sins, for we ourselves forgive everyone who is indebted to us. And lead us not into temptation." (Luke 11:1–4 ESV)

"And lead us not into temptation but deliver us from evil: For thine is the kingdom, and the power, and the glory, forever. Amen." (Matthew 6:13 KJV)

"And Peter answered him, "Lord, if it is you, command me to come to you on the water." He said, "Come." So Peter got out of the boat and walked on the water and came to Jesus. But when he saw the wind, he was afraid, and beginning to sink he cried out, "Lord, save me." Jesus immediately reached out his hand and took hold of him, saying to him, "O you of little faith, why did you doubt?" And when they got into the boat, the wind ceased." (Matthew 14:28–32 ESV)

These scriptures emphasize that God seeks connection with us and can work miracles for and through us if we ask. Prayer is essential, and Dr. Larry Lea's approach to the Disciples' Prayer, or Lord's Prayer, follows the outline Jesus provided.

LARRY LEA'S PRAYER GUIDE: SETTING A PRAYERFUL HORIZON ON THE DISCIPLES' PRAYER

(Matt. 6:9, KJV) "After this manner therefore pray ye: Our Father which art in heaven, hallowed be thy name."[4]

What should a typical conversation with God be like? What should it include?

I. "Our Father which art in heaven, hallowed be Thy Name…" (Matt. 6:9)

   a. Picture Calvary and thank God; you can call Him our Father by virtue of the blood of Jesus.

   b. Hallow the names of God corresponding with the benefits in the New Covenant.

MAKE YOUR FAITH DECLARATIONS.

BENEFIT	NAME	MEANING
Sin	Jehovah-Tsidkenu	The Lord, my Righteousness
	Jehovah-M'Kaddesh	The Lord Who Sanctifies
Spirit	Jehovah-shalom	The Lord is Peace
	Jehovah-Shammah	The Lord Who is there
Soundness	Jehovah-Rophe/Rapha	The Lord Who heals
Success	Jehovah-Jireh	The Lord, my Provider
	Jehovah-Nissi	The Lord my Banner
Security	Jehovah- Rohi	The Lord, my Shepherd

II. "Thy kingdom come, thy will be done on earth as it is in heaven…"

[4] Larry Lea, 189.

a. Your family (yourself, spouse, children, other family members).
b. Your church (pastor, leadership, faithfulness of the people, harvest, etc.).
c. Nation (city, state, and national political and spiritual leaders, a specific nation).
d. The nations (pick a nation; pray for Israel daily.

III. "Give us this day our daily bread…"

a. Be in the will of God (prayer life, church, work, habits, obedience in giving).
b. Believe it is God's will to prosper you.
c. Be specific.
d. Be tenacious.

IV. "And forgive us our trespasses, as we forgive those who trespass against us…"

a. Forgive yourself.
b. Forgive and release others.
c. Set your will to forgive those who sinned against you.

V. "And lead us not into temptation but deliver us from evil…" Put on the whole armor of God, the Lord Jesus Christ.

1. Loins girt about with truth.
2. Breastplate of righteousness.

3. Feet shod with the preparation (readiness) of the gospel of peace.
4. Shield of faith.
5. Helmet of salvation.
6. Sword of the Spirit, which is the Word (rhema) of God.
7. Praying always in the Spirit.

VI. Pray a hedge of protection (the Lord is your refuge, your fortress, your God, in Him you will trust).

1. Because you have made the Lord your habitation.
2. Because you have set your love upon Him.
3. Because you have known His name.

VII. "For Thine is the kingdom, and the power, and the glory forever."

1. Make your faith declaration.
2. Return to praise.

CRITICAL STEPS LESSON 1:

"Far better is it to dare mighty things, to win glorious triumphs, even though checkered by failure, than to take rank with those poor spirits who neither enjoy much nor suffer much because they live in the grey twilight that knows neither victory nor defeat." – Theodore Roosevelt 26th President of the United States.

WORSHIP:

1. We should trust God completely. He is sovereign and always keeps His Word (Rom. 4:20).
2. We should bear fruit (John 15:8).
3. We should have an expressed attitude of gratitude (Heb. 13:16).

PRAYER:

1. We should pray in faith (Mark 11:24).
2. We should pray with authority (John 14:13).
3. We should pray specifically (James 4:2).
4. We should pray with proper motives (James 4:3).

OBEDIENCE:

We should make the commitment to take God at His Word and what He tells us in it. We should know God's Word. This happens best through: A.P.R.O.V.E.

a. Affirmation-Prayerfully (Matt. 6:9-13).
b. Preparation-Ask God (James 1:5).
c. Revelation-After reading Scripture, consult commentaries and helps (2 Tim. 2:15).
d. Observation-Read your Bible daily and systematically (1 Tim. 4:13).

e. Verification-Carefully analyze Scripture. Your Bible study is not finished until you have applied what you learned.

CLOSING THE GAP ON LESSON 1

Peter, when overwhelmed by his fear, uttered the shortest prayer in the Bible. In light of the risky situations ahead, each person says how they would like their group to pray for them. Six months from now, my life will reflect this promise; in light of a current risky situation, I will choose to look at Jesus instead of the waves.

Date in 6 months: ______________

QUESTIONS FOR REFLECTION

1. For a fisherman like Peter, his boat had to be everything. Why did Jesus call Peter out of his boat?
2. What do you think went through Peter's mind while walking on water?
3. Why does the lord push us into risky situations?
4. What caused this confident water walker to start swallowing water?

In Group, PRAY 5-10 min. daily for the needs of group members.

WRAP-UP DISCUSSION:

Personal evaluation on your own (discuss next week).

On a scale of 1-10, rate yourself in the following areas:

1. I have committed my life totally to Jesus Christ. ___
2. I am involved in worshipping God according to the biblical pattern. ___
3. I am committed to Pray until Something Happens. ___
4. My word is my bond. ___
5. God's Word is my source of faith and rule of conduct. ___
6. I will commit to telling this group next week how my faith has been strengthened.

CHAPTER 2

A DISCIPLE AND THE WORD OF GOD

A DISCIPLE IS COMMITTED TO PRACTICING THE WORD THROUGH SPIRITUAL INTEGRITY, MORALITY, and ETHICAL PURITY

Temptation

If anyone thinks that they will not be tempted, they are not thinking biblically. The text tells us we will be tempted in all ways, but that with temptation, God will give us some means of escape.

> *No temptation has overtaken you that is not common to man. God is faithful, and he will not let you be tempted beyond your ability, but with the temptation, he will also provide a way of escape that you may be able to endure it. (1 Cor. 10:13)*

I have encountered failures in life and more will likely come. Failure in a Christian walk differs from failure in a worldly walk. Claiming to be without failure would be dishonest: *if we say we have not sinned, we make him a liar, and his word is not in us (1 John 1:10).* The types of failures we deal with as believers are more along the biblical view of the lack of things, such as not reading the Bible, prayerlessness, the lack of faith, the lack of fellowship, and worldliness.

I do not deny that believers still fail and fall into the other types of sins, i.e., lust of the flesh, lust of the eyes, the pride of life, and other things that we see in the scriptural text. The book of Galatians gives us an entire list (Gal 5:19-21). Not to mention the fact that many of us are very poor witnesses of the kingdom to our neighbors and coworkers. When believers fail, the biblical text is our reality check for conviction.

What does the Text say?

When I think of conviction related to the biblical text, I think of one of my college professors. He was an accomplished author of several books on the Holy Spirit, with whom I had become more closely acquainted after the death of his wife.

One day, he came to me and said, "Jim, let's go have a cup of coffee, I need answers to a dilemma that I'm having." He knew I had been a hospice chaplain, and he was sure I knew about something he was experiencing. He said, "I have been seeing my wife who passed away recently. Jim, I want to know, am I going crazy, or is this real?"

My colleague always reminded us that when we asked questions, especially in a biblical or theological context, we should also ask, "What does the text say?" Here I was, giving my mentor advice about what the text says about his experience. So, I asked him that very question. "What does the text say about your situation?"

As we were discussing several scriptural evidences of encounters similar to his, we see the one biblical text giving us instructions of what we are to do in encounters like this. Sometimes people seek that which is not of God to get answers to a dilemma, as we see with King Saul in 1 Samuel 28.

> *Then Saul said to his servants, "Seek out for me a woman who is a medium, that I may go to her and inquire of her." And his servants said to him, "Behold, there is a medium at En-dor. (1 Samuel 28:7)*

King Saul went to a medium to seek advice from the prophet Samuel, who had passed away. This was a demonic intervention. I truly believe that my friend's inquiry came from a conviction related to textual issues. It was not so much about him losing his mind than it was his mind being influenced by demons. He was not in a position of losing his kingdom, or his position as a professor, but I believe he was confronted by a demon. This shows you so much about understanding the scriptural text and what we need to do to encounter answers from God. If we are convicted with what the text says, we will always get our answer.

Answers to questions like the one asked by my colleague can only be found in the biblical text. The Holy Spirit should be the primary method for understanding what we experience in our walk with God. As a hospice chaplain, I knew people that had visitations from Jesus and angels. Some individuals had even seen glimpses of and had visits to heaven. Anything else would be independent of the biblical knowledge that we have. We do know that Satan appears as an angel of light (2 Corinthians 11:14).

As we look further, I see two examples that come forth out of the biblical text regarding King David and Apostle Paul. Both instances are concerning the role of the Holy Spirit and what different scenarios can arise when we are seeking answers in our daily life. Scenarios arise that prompt believers to ask, was it God, or was it the devil?

David was considered a man after God's own heart *(Acts 13:22).* He saw Bathsheba and decided, after not so much of a debate (conviction), with himself, to not just look and admire her beauty. He inquired who she was, and then he wanted her for himself. Was it because he was king who had everything available to him and everyone submissive to him? Or was it because he was also a man, who in this instance was controlled by his flesh?

To say we will not be tempted is to deny with the scripture that in James 1:13-15 says:

> *Let no one say when he is tempted, 'I am being tempted by God,' for God cannot be tempted with evil, and he himself tempts no one. But each person is tempted when he is lured and enticed by his own desire Then desire when it has conceived gives birth to sin, and sin when it is fully grown brings forth death. (Jas 1:13–15).*

The Holy Spirit's ministry forever covers us because Jesus said he would never leave you or forsake you. He promised to send us the Holy Spirit, who would accomplish three things in our lives: convicting the world of sin, righteousness and judgment.

> *And when he, i.e., the Holy Spirit, comes, he will convict the world concerning sin and righteousness and judgment: concerning sin, because they do not believe in me; concerning righteousness, because I go to the Father, and you will see me no longer; concerning judgment, because the ruler of this world is judged. (John 16:8–11 ESV)*

David was convicted by the Holy Spirit when Nathan confronted him. Everyone, regardless of belief, makes choices in life influenced by these three prompts from the Holy Spirit. David's choice could have been altered by his conviction of right or wrong to not have an affair with another man's wife.

The Apostle Paul is another example of this conviction. According to the text, he was designated as an instrument to serve as a witness to the Gentiles, though he was initially unaware of this role (Acts 9:15). He previously persecuted Christians, having received letters authorizing action against them. This changed when he encountered Jesus on the road to Damascus.

> *Now as he went on his way, he approached Damascus, and suddenly a light from heaven shone around him. And falling to the ground, he heard a voice saying to him, 'Saul, Saul, why are you persecuting me?' And he said, 'Who are you, Lord?' And he said, 'I am Jesus, whom you are persecuting. But rise and enter the city, and you will be told what you are to do. (Acts 9:3–6)*

Luke intended his readers to understand this as an observable event. While it was aimed at Paul, the companions traveling with Paul *heard the sound* even *if they did not see anyone.*[5]

Ananias, a disciple of Jesus Christ, was instructed by the Lord concerning Apostle Saul:

> *But the Lord said to him, 'Go, for he is a chosen instrument of mine to carry my name before the Gentiles and kings and the children of Israel. (Acts 9:15)*

Ananias's acceptance of this tenuous situation and placing of *his hands on Saul* was a gesture expressing recognition and confirmation of God's acceptance and Christian unity, as was the greeting, *Brother Saul.*

In Saul's case the laying on of hands and God's acceptance were tied up with his healing, his reception of the Holy Spirit and baptism and even with the breaking of his fast. All these things happened together. Perhaps it is also significant that they happened independently of the Jerusalem apostles (9:26-27).[6]

After committing to follow Jesus, my sense of purpose became more evident, bearing a strong resemblance to the transformative experience described as the Damascus Road encounter. The audible voice of God that I heard in service that Sunday reminded me of the Apostle's experience.

---

[5] Conrad Gempf, *Acts*, ed. D. A Carson et al., New Bible Commentary: 21st Century Edition. Accordance electronic ed. (Downers Grove: InterVarsity Press, 1994), 1079.

[6] Conrad Gempf, *Acts*, ed. D. A Carson et al., New Bible Commentary: 21st Century Edition. Accordance electronic ed. (Downers Grove: InterVarsity Press, 1994), 1079.

My grandmother, Pearl Barber, would always take me to church with her. I'll never forget getting in the backseat of Mr. Lim's Chrysler Desoto, and hearing Grandma say, "Jimmy, you're gonna be a preacher one day."

To me, "Preacher" carried the connotations of those fat men, sweating and slobbering with a handkerchief and wiping their foreheads and mustaches. It was not appealing to me.

However, that October 17, 1982, *180-degree turning point* was a change; it was a powerful calling. I came face-to-face with the Lord Jesus Christ in the church that Sunday when the minister quoted Matthew 18:19.

The Geiger counter in my life did a flip. I had never heard God's voice, nor had I ever walked an aisle on a Sunday morning in a church, but I became a disciple of the Lord Jesus Christ that day. I wanted to read his word, follow him, and learn all I could of his life and how he walked with the men and women that he called. I had become what one of my seminary professors, Dr. Snow, has phrased it, "A disciple is a loyal, learning follower of Jesus Christ." I had become that person. I no longer wanted the things I used to long for, the lust of my flesh, the lust of my eyes, or pride any longer. I wanted Jesus.

The following lesson for this chapter will help the reader to see the need for practicing the word of God through spiritual integrity, morality, & ethical purity. The conviction of the Holy Spirit that we discussed in this chapter should become more evident in every individual's life. Practicing the word of God is not hard. We just have to do what it says.

Lesson for Chapter 2

A Disciple and The Word of God

A DISCIPLE IS COMMITTED TO PRACTICING THE WORD THROUGH SPIRITUAL INTEGRITY, MORALITY, and ETHICAL PURITY

CORE ISSUE: PURITY

KEY PASSAGE: *"Now it is required that those who have been given a trust must prove faithful." (1 Cor. 4:2)*

WARM-UP DISCUSSION:

Living in a culture dominated by sensuality, nearly every day, we are subject to possible temptations that could lead us toward immorality. Regularly, we read of another prominent leader who falls into sexual sin. What causes someone to sell out his or her reputation so cheaply?

BACKGROUND

Joseph was the youngest of 12 children. At the age of 17, he was sold into slavery by his own brothers and taken to Egypt. God had a plan for this young man that placed him in a highly responsible position in the palace of Egypt's pharaoh. Joseph was only in his 20s in Genesis 39, but he showed wisdom well beyond his years.

LET'S READ THE WORD: Gen. 39:3-23

His master saw that the LORD was with him and that the LORD caused all that he did to succeed in his hands. So Joseph found favor in his sight and attended him, and he made him overseer of his house and put him in charge of all that he had. From the time that he made him overseer in his house and over all that he had, the LORD blessed the Egyptian's house for Joseph's sake; the blessing of the LORD was on all that he had, in house and field. So he left all that he had in Joseph's charge, and because of him he had no concern about anything but the food he ate.

Now Joseph was handsome in form and appearance. And after a time his master's wife cast her eyes on Joseph and said, "Lie with me." But he refused and said to his master's wife, "Behold, because of me my master has no concern about anything in the house, and he has put everything that he has in my charge. He is not greater in this house than I am, nor has he kept back anything from me except you, because you are his wife. How then can I do this great wickedness and sin against God?" And as she spoke to Joseph day after day, he would not listen to her, to lie beside her or to be with her.

But one day, when he went into the house to do his work and none of the men of the house was there in the house, she caught him by his garment, saying, "Lie with me." But he left his garment in her hand and fled and got out of the house. And as soon as she saw that he had left his garment in her hand and had fled out of the house, she called to the men of her household and said to them, "See, he has brought among us a Hebrew to laugh at us. He came in to me to lie with me, and I cried out with a loud voice. And as soon as he heard that I lifted up my voice and cried out, he left his garment beside me and fled and got out of the house." Then she laid up his garment by her until his master came home and she told him the same story, saying, "The Hebrew servant, whom you have brought among us, came in to me to laugh at me. But as soon as I lifted up my voice and cried, he left his garment beside me and fled out of the house."

As soon as his master heard the words that his wife spoke to him, "This is the way your servant treated me," his anger was kindled. And Joseph's master took him and put him into the prison, the place where the king's prisoners were confined, and he was there in prison. But the LORD was with Joseph and showed him steadfast love and gave him favor in the sight of the keeper of the prison. And the keeper of the prison put Joseph in charge of all the prisoners who were in prison. Whatever was done there, he was the one who did it. The keeper of the prison paid no attention to anything that was in Joseph's charge, because the LORD was with him. And whatever he did, the LORD made it succeed.

CRITICAL STEPS LESSON 2

SPIRITUAL PURITY:

1. Bring every thought under the control of Jesus (2 Cor. 10:3-5).
2. Set a specific time to spend with the Lord. Ask Him to help you to be consistent.
3. Each morning, ask for victory in your weak areas and to keep you from all temptation (Matt. 6:13).
4. Commit your day to the Lord. Ask him to give you His thoughts, His words to speak, his expressions on your face, and to be glorified in all you do and say (Ps. 37:5, 6).
5. Take spiritual authority in your family, leading them in the ways of the Lord and spending time with them.

MORAL PURITY:

1. In your quiet time, ask the Lord to keep you pure for this day, to control your thoughts, to show you temptation, and how to resist the temptation.
2. When temptation comes, determine that you should:
    a. Flee from it (1 Cor. 6:18; 2 Tim. 2:22).
    b. Resist by diverting your mind to other things, such as praising the Lord (Jas. 4:7).
    c. Claim 1 Cor. 10:13 "No temptation has seized you except what is common to man. And God is faithful;

he will not let you be tempted beyond what you can bear. But when you are tempted, he will also provide a way out so that you can stand up under it."

d. And Phil. 4:13: "I can do everything through him who gives me strength."

ETHICAL PURITY:

1. Do a study on the faithfulness of God, noting how He honors those who follow His ways (Job, Joseph, Daniel, and his three friends).
2. Commit to the Lord not to compromise in any area, no matter the pressures or consequences (Ps. 119:36: "Turn my heart toward your statutes and not toward selfish gain"; Matt. 6:33: "But seek first his kingdom and his righteousness, and all these things will be given to you as well.").
3. Ask the Lord to give you Scripture to apply to areas in which you currently are tempted to compromise.
4. Let a friend hold you accountable in your weak areas (Prov. 27:6: "Faithful are the wounds of a friend, but deceitful are the kisses of an enemy").
5. Seek the advice of older, Spirit-filled believers who may have insights on how to resist compromise.
6. Meditate on 1 Cor. 8:9: "Be careful, however, that the exercise of your freedom does not become a stumbling block to the weak."

QUESTIONS FOR INTERACTION:

1. Why did Joseph's boss trust him so totally?
2. What made Joseph so desirable to this man's wife?
3. Why was Joseph so vulnerable to her sexual advances?
4. What makes us vulnerable?
5. If Joseph were in our group here, how might we have helped him in dealing with the advances of the boss' wife?
6. What were Joseph's reasons for saying no?
7. What enabled him to move from reason to responsible action?

WRAP-UP DISCUSSION CLOSING THE GAP ON LESSON 2:

1. Is it possible for a Christian to live a godly, pure life in today's "pressure-cooker" society?
2. Why or why not?
3. What signals does a person that is attracted to you emit? Talk together about how this group can help each other say "no."
4. What have you learned since last week to do about sexual lust and temptation, since most of us rarely outgrow our sexual passions?
5. Lord willing, six months from now, my life will reflect this lesson. Date: ______________

Personal Evaluation on your own.

On a scale of 1-10

(1 = Totally disagree & 10 = Totally agree).

Please rate yourself in the following:

1. I know where my line is—that is, where I'm in danger morally. ___
2. I am giving things to the Lord that will help me become more faithful to Him. ___
3. My thought life is well-controlled. ___
4. My eyes will not wander where they should not go. ___
5. I am faithful in doing what is right, even with "the little things." ___
6. As for sexual purity, that area of my life is totally under control. ___

CHAPTER 3

A Disciple and Their Mentors and Friends

A DISCIPLE IS COMMITTED TO PURSUING VITAL RELATIONSHIPS WITH A FEW OTHERS, UNDERSTANDING THE NEED TO HELP EACH OTHER KEEP THEIR PROMISES

Many churches lack sufficient teaching on following Jesus. This lack can leave a church body with feelings of isolation, discontent, and a reduced willingness to volunteer for the needs of the church community. The church has failed to develop the key areas of discipleship that include Prayer, Word, Fellowship, and Evangelism. These areas are, at best, taught inconsistently, and at worst, nonexistent.

This lack of purposeful discipleship affects all areas of a believer's life. Without accountability and fellowship, the feeling of isolation and a lack of commitment to the Word of God and its teachings can be devastating. This is particularly true in the life of the new and immature believer that can make them feel purposeless and directionless without someone to pour into their lives. The Word on the inside can stagnate when no one stimulates or gives someone the opportunity to share.

The need in the church today is for the development of a process designed to provide discipleship principles and encourage men and women to meet regularly to begin developing the vital characteristics that make them whole and mature believers. Men and women who are discipled will become better lay workers and leaders in their church, more committed in their homes and their marriages, more dynamic in their communities, and more effective in their world.

Through the benefits of prayer, the study of the Word of God, personal group fellowship, and evangelism, the needs of the church can be actualized. They will fortify individual opportunities to give and receive ministry. These four things are what is required to obtain what Leroy Eims describes as disciple making:

> The ministry is to be carried on by people, not programs. It is to be carried out by someone and not by some other thing. Disciples cannot be mass produced. We cannot drop people into a "program" and see disciples emerge at the end of the production line. It takes time to make disciples. It takes individual, personal attention. It takes hours of prayer for them. It takes patience and understanding to teach them how to get into the Word of God for themselves, how to feed and nourish their souls, and by the power of the Holy Spirit how to apply the word to their lives. And it takes being an example to them of all of the above.[7]

[7] LeRoy Eims, *The Lost Art of Disciple Making* (Grand Rapids, MI: Zondervan, 1978), 45-46, Kindle Edition.

He illustrates this fact by comparing the Church with a shoe-making factory that worked assiduously for two years but manufactured no shoes. "That's right, the manager says, no shoes, but we are really busy. In fact, we have been so busy that we are all nearly tired out."[8]

This scenario aptly describes churches that have been so caught up in producing programs and developing materials they have become complacent regarding the discipling process.

The Great Commission calls the Church to make disciples, not just converts.

> *And Jesus came and said to them, "All authority in heaven and on earth has been given to me. Go therefore and make disciples of all nations, baptizing them in the name of the Father and of the Son and of the Holy Spirit, teaching them to observe all that I have commanded you. And behold, I am with you always, to the end of the age. (Matthew 28:18-20)*

How disciples are made today will depend partly on each man's gift and role in society; however, everyone who believes and follows after Christ is called to the function of discipling, whether it falls within one's vocation or not. Eims intimates that most men have never been in a formal relationship with a more mature Christian who guides them step-by-step in the process of growth as a disciple of Jesus Christ. That is the problem this project seeks to address.[9]

---

[8] Leroy Eims, 46.
[9] Leroy Eims, 46.

Pastors Bob & Sue Farrar

One Sunday morning in 1984, while sitting in the congregation at COTR, I had the following thoughts as Senior Pastor Dr. Larry Lea was sharing about involvement in the church. The thought that came to me was:

> Could God use an individual with a checkered past that included sex, drugs, and divorce? Could such a person really have purpose and meaning in the Kingdom of God? Could a theology that was embedded in one's thinking that says that a history of depraved living would be offensive to God and, therefore, could never be used by Him. Could a belief system that divorce is an unforgivable sin prevent someone from following the call of God in their life? Is there enough grace and mercy to make room for a person who left that lifestyle and is now living a new life?

At that very moment, I believe God heard those thoughts, and He sent an answer. A young woman invited me to attend the Single Adult Sunday School Class. When I asked the rhetorical question: "Why should I attend such a meeting?", she explained that the Single Adult Pastors, Bob and Sue Farrar, were having a tremendous impact on many single men and women in the church through their dynamic teaching on relationships. Their caring insight and personal involvement changed many lives of these single men and women.

In my mind, it seemed unthinkable to become involved in a group of single, mostly divorced individuals who were apparently without purpose, or were looking for the next failed relationship. The mention of the Farrars continued to come up during a cell group meeting of an older adult woman from COTR that I worked with at "The Club." I also heard their names a few times during announcements at services.

After several weeks, I became curious to see what was going on in this Singles Group and with the Farrars. The ministry of this couple became pivotal for my life when Sue Farrar gave a prophetic word of knowledge during the first meeting that I attended. 1 Corinthians 12:8 refers to this ability of the Holy Spirit to know facts about a situation that could not have been known by natural means. This was during a Sunday morning class meeting when Pastor Sue spoke the following prophetic word:

> I would like all of the men named James to stand up. God has a specific word for several of you, and He has a word, especially for someone named James or several men named James. Today, the Lord is calling you out of your death, like the call to Lazarus, who was bound up and dead. His hands and feet were bound with grave clothes, and his face also. I am this day saying to you put off those grave clothes, be set free, and come forth out of the grave. He is crying out to you, just as He did to Lazarus, to come forth. If that is you, I want you to come to the altar; I want to pray for you.

I was not going to stand, but there were about 4 or 5 who stood, so I did also. It was a specific, penetrating word. It felt as if she had looked inside of my thoughts. I couldn't believe it could possibly be for me, but she was talking about how I felt. I was new to the charismatic movement, so the gifts of the Spirit were new, but it was also refreshing to hear my situation as a concern of God through the Holy Spirit.

Gradually, I became more involved in the class and the singles ministry at COTR. Pastor Bob Farrar later cemented my turning point when he challenged everyone in the singles ministry to become disciples. He asked us to make a commitment to the Lord Jesus Christ and each other. This sealed the prophetic word given by Pastor Sue and prompted me and others to make a covenant change that would require hard work in prayer, scripture reading, and memory lessons.

The Design for Discipleship, published by The Navigators[10] was one of the premiere pieces of teaching on discipleship in the churches at the time. It was being used as our model to learn and grow as disciples of Jesus Christ.

While we were participating in the Navigators course, I became involved with a cell group with James (Jim) Schwartz, who was one of the James' who stood, and became one of my close friends. After several months, Jim began to see that I had the potential to be a cell leader. So, I multiplied a new group out of Jim's group. Several people went with me in the multiplication process from Jim's group.

The principle of multiplication is fantastic because it apportions your church up into teams. I am reminded of Jethro coming to Moses when he was trying to minister to the millions of people who were with him in the wilderness. The division of groups was an awesome process that all churches should begin to see as an Old and New Testament pattern for church growth and care of the body. Exodus 18:13-23 helps us to understand the principle that Jethro gave Moses.

10 The Navigators, *Design for Discipleship Series: Set of 7 Guides plus Leader's Guide* (CO: NavPress, 1973).

Lesson for Chapter 3

A Disciple and their Mentors and Friends

A DISCIPLE IS COMMITTED TO PURSUING VITAL RELATIONSHIPS WITH A FEW OTHERS, UNDERSTANDING THE NEED TO HELP EACH OTHER KEEP THEIR PROMISES

CORE ISSUE: UNITY

KEY PASSAGE:

> *...Not neglecting to meet together, as is the habit of some, but encouraging one another, and all the more as you see the Day drawing near. (Heb. 10:25)*

WARM-UP DISCUSSION: *(Fictional)*

As Ralph and Sue drove across the new bridge, they marveled at the way it reduced traffic and shaved off minutes of their morning commute to downtown. However, building bridges between people makes an even greater impact on the lives of our country and our world. Sometimes, we can build bridges into new relationships, and often, we need to rebuild the bridges of an existing relationship. In your life, what have been some of the causes of broken relationships? What have we seen work to fix them?

BACKGROUND

Building bridges with the people around us is a challenge, especially when we would like to introduce them to Jesus. Moreover, for people we know, such as family and friends, it is even more difficult. Where do we begin? In addition, how do we know they are interested in the first place? The Apostle Paul was a master of building bridges. Let us look at how he made relationships possible.

LET'S READ THE WORD: 1 Cor. 9:19-23

For though I am free from all, I have made myself a servant to all, that I might win more of them. To the Jews I became a Jew, in order to win Jews. To those under the law I became as one under the law (though not being myself under the law) that I might win those under the law. To those outside the law I became as one outside the law (not being outside the law of God but under the law of Christ) that I might win those outside the law. To the weak I became weak, that I might win the weak. I have become all things to all people, that by all means I might save some. I do it all for the sake of the gospel, that I may share with them in its blessings.

QUESTIONS FOR INTERACTION:

1. What is necessary to connect with people different than us if we hope to have a relationship with them?

2. Why would anyone want to build a bridge with someone beyond cultural and racial barriers? (v. 19)
3. How would you describe Paul's motivation for making relationships across such a broad spectrum?

CLOSING THE GAP ON LESSON 3

Can you identify one or more types of the fellowships in your life? *(One or two people can fulfill all 3 roles.)*

1. A Paul ____________________ An older person building into your life.
2. A Barnabas ____________________ A soul brother/sister to keep you accountable.
3. A Timothy ____________________ A newbie into whose life you build.

Can you identify one or more of the close disciple types in your life? (One or two people can fulfill all 3 roles.)

1. A Peter __________________________ Directs You.
2. A James __________________________ Leads You.
3. A John __________________________ Loves You.

Personal Evaluation on your own:

The golden rule applies directly to building strong relationships. To find and keep friends, you must be a friend. Jesus said do unto others as you would have them do unto you (Luke 6:31). We begin a mentoring relationship by asking ourselves how we like to be treated. Start with these ideas about yourself:

I will identify people who are inside and outside my comfort zone and begin to look for opportunities to meet them and learn at least their names.

WRAP-UP DISCUSSION:

____ **Acceptance** – I want to be fully known and accepted for who I am without becoming someone's project.

____ **Understanding** – I want to be listened to without interruption and unsolicited advice.

____ **Loyalty** – I want others to keep confidence without ever wanting to hurt me or others.

____ **Self-disclosure** – I want to risk revealing my innermost feelings without fear of rejection or manipulation.

____ **Availability** – I want others to be there for me or others, night or day, in time of need.

____ **Genuineness** – I want people to be who and what they say they are.

Take five minutes and evaluate yourself related to the six key practices of relationships above based on your past, others, or self. Place your response in the space provided. On a scale of 1-10, rate yourself:

1. Being the lowest, I don't want to or can't. *(Influenced by past, self, others)* ____
2. Being: I want to, but **feel** I can't. *(Influenced by self)* ____

3. Being: I want to, but **fear** what **others** think. *(Influenced by others)* ____
4. Being: I want to, but know I **won't /can't** finish. *(Influenced by past)* ____
5. Being the midpoint, I do want to, but I have **fear and doubt**. *(Influenced by past, self, others)* ____
6. Being; I do, but I have a fear of what **others** think. *(Influenced by others)* ____
7. Being; I do, but I have doubts that I'll be **accepted**. *(Influenced by others)* ____
8. Being; I do, but I don't know if I **really** want to. *(Influenced by self)* ____
9. Being; I do want to, but I **think** I will have a hard time. *(Influenced by past)* ____
10. Being the highest, **I do, and I want to**. *(Influenced by past, self, others)* ____

Be honest. As like attracts like, you will find what you attract in someone else is also in you. Lord willing, six months from now, my life will reflect this promise. Date: ______________

Prayer Request: PRAY 5-10 min. daily for the needs of group members. List prayer requests for each other's needs below. Note answers to prayers.

____

____

CHAPTER 4

A Disciple and their Family and Relationships

A DISCIPLE IS COMMITTED TO A STRONG FAMILY AND PERSONAL RELATIONSHIPS THROUGH LOVE, PROTECTIONS, AND BIBLICAL VALUES

Realized Fellowship

> *Not neglecting to meet together, as is the habit of some, but encouraging one another, and all the more as you see the Day drawing near. (Hebrews. 10:25)*

Without affirmation, family-type relationships, and fellowship, the feeling of isolation that results can cause a lack of commitment to the Word of God and its teachings, particularly in the life of the new and immature believer. As a result, many believers can feel the season to be purposeless and directionless without someone to pour themselves into or for others to pour into their lives. This is one of the dilemmas that we have during a holiday.

I have always believed that family and relationships are of the utmost importance in a person's life. My family was very tight. We had gatherings and get-togethers to celebrate holidays, birthdays, and church events. There was a rare thing that we did not do regularly, but other families did, called in the Black community, the "Family Reunions." My family did not celebrate many of these. We had get-togethers, but not regularly like some Black families.

My parents were actively part of what was called Social Clubs. These clubs would travel to the beach and the mountains and have events at the regional theme parks and at the lakes around the state, which really solidified fellowship among church believers and family.

I called this "Realized Fellowship," which always began with God, as most Black Americans had a central relationship with the church. These relationships extended from the church into the community. It touched almost every individual in the community and influenced the lifestyle in what could be referred to as community discipleship. Everybody knew the pastors in the community, everyone encouraged each other in these small community relationships. My mom would always say anybody in the community could beat your butt if they knew you. This was the concept of family that I called "Realized Fellowship."

Realized fellowship that begins with God and flows to other individuals is similar to family fellowship, seen in the lifestyle of a disciple. F. F. Bruce, writing about the first disciples, explains that the twelve arrived at their final intimate relationship and fellowship with Jesus by degrees. There were three distinct stages in their development. They began as simple believers and occasional companions at convenient times, particularly during festive seasons. Fellowship followed in interrupted attendance, even to the abandonment of their secular vocations. Finally, they were set apart by their master as certain disciples.[11]

The twelve experienced a discipling process that fostered a definite change in their behavior. While Christian discipleship requires obedience, it is not simply a discipline of works. Leslie Weatherhead remarks that the normal life of the Christian is a life of fellowship. Fellowshipping with other believers is walking in obedience because a normal and full Christian life cannot be lived alone.[12]

Ray Stedman, in *Body Life*, emphasizes this fellowship element as well. He reiterates the point that as an essential part of early Christianity, this fellowship element is still necessary today.[13] Eims also believes that a growing Christian needs fellowship, which is one of the basic needs of a growing Christian church.

Like family, the body of Christ is not a group of people in one building like marbles in a bag but like lumps of chocolate that have melted together and become part of one another.[14] This emphasizes both the relationships of believers with one another and the relationship of believers with God. Inwardly, people must be motivated to have fellowship with Jesus Christ, and outwardly, they must become witnesses to Jesus Christ.

---

[11] A. B. Bruce, *The Training of the Twelve* (Grand Rapids, MI: Kregel, 1971), 11-12.
[12] Leslie Weatherhead, *Discipleship* (London: SCM Press, 1958), 63.
[13] Ray Stedman, *Body Life,* (Glendale: Regal, 1972), 107.
[14] Eims, 64.

Lesson for Chapter 4

A Disciple and their Family and Relationships

A DISCIPLE IS COMMITTED TO A STRONG FAMILY AND PERSONAL RELATIONSHIPS THROUGH LOVE, PROTECTIONS, AND BIBLICAL VALUES

CORE ISSUE: SERVANTHOOD

KEY PASSAGE:

Matt. 20:26-27, NIV "...Whoever wants to become great among you must be your servant, (Greek. Minister Servant) and whoever wants to be first must be your slave," -- (Greek Bond Servant)

WARM-UP DISCUSSION *(Fictional)*

When Jeff was just a boy, his grandfather promised, "Someday, I will take you to our family roots in Germany." Jeff grew up excited about someday making that trip. Grandpa didn't take his own promises as seriously as did his grandson, however. The trip never happened. Recall a promise made to you that was kept or broken.

BACKGROUND

David had served as Israel's king for about seven years. The highlight of his formative years had been his relationship with Jonathan, son of the former king, Saul. David and Jonathan had made a promise to take care of each other's households should something happen to either of them. Jonathan said to David,

> *. . . and remember, you must demonstrate the love and kindness of the Lord not only to me during my lifetime, but also to my children after the Lord has destroyed all of your enemies. (1Sam. 20:15, LB)*

One day, David began wondering if any of Saul's family was still living, for David wanted to be kind to them, just as he had promised.

LET'S READ THE TEXT: 2 Sam. 9: 1 – 13

> *And David said, 'Is there still anyone left of the house of Saul, that I may show him kindness for Jonathan's sake?' Now there was a servant of the house of Saul whose name was Ziba, and they called him to David. And the king said to him, 'Are you Ziba?' And he said, 'I am your servant.' And the king said, 'Is there not still someone of the house of Saul, that I may show the kindness of God to him?' Ziba said to the king, 'There is still a son of Jonathan; he is crippled in his feet.' The king said to him, 'Where is he?' And Ziba said to the king, 'He is in the house of Machir the son of Ammiel, at Lo-debar.' Then King David sent and brought him from the house of Machir the son of Ammiel, at Lo-debar. And Mephibosheth the son of Jonathan, son*

> *of Saul, came to David and fell on his face and paid homage. And David said, 'Mephibosheth!' And he answered, 'Behold, I am your servant.' And David said to him, 'Do not fear, for I will show you kindness for the sake of your father Jonathan, and I will restore to you all the land of Saul your father, and you shall eat at my table always.' And he paid homage and said, 'What is your servant, that you should show regard for a dead dog such as I?'*
>
> *Then the king called Ziba, Saul's servant, and said to him, 'All that belonged to Saul and to all his house I have given to your master's grandson. And you and your sons and your servants shall till the land for him and shall bring in the produce, that your master's grandson may have bread to eat. But Mephibosheth your master's grandson shall always eat at my table.' Now Ziba had fifteen sons and twenty servants. Then Ziba said to the king, 'According to all that my lord the king commands his servant, so will your servant do.' So Mephibosheth ate at David's table, like one of the king's sons. And Mephibosheth had a young son, whose name was Mica. And all who lived in Ziba's house became Mephibosheth's servants. So Mephibosheth lived in Jerusalem, for he ate always at the king's table. Now he was lame in both his feet.*

IN YOUR FAMILY, MARRIAGE, OR RELATIONSHIPS

If you are married, in a family, or any relationship (Church, Work, School), talk with the people connected to you and let them know how important they are to your life. Encourage them to see God's provision and solution for every concern (Rom. 8:28; Phil. 4:19). How?

Spend *quality* time with the people you care about doing things they like.

> *And let us not neglect our meeting together, as some people do, but encourage and warn each other, especially now that the day of his coming back again is drawing near. (Hebrews 10:25 NLT)*

Through Love

- Keep your *promises* (James 5:12).
- Let them know you are *praying* for them (Rom. 1:9, 10).
- Instruct them in a *nurturing* way (Ephesians 6:4).
- *Assure* them that you are proud of them.

Providing Protection

- Teach them how to *recognize* and *avoid* dangers (Proverbs 3).
- Pray a *hedge* of protection around them (Job 3:23; Psalm 34:19).
- Teach them to ask the Lord for *protection* and wisdom at all times (Proverbs 3:5-8; James 1: 5-8).

Using Biblical Values

- Help them to *respect* and honor God in all they do (Proverbs 1:7).
- *Model* and instill godly *standards* and discipline.
- Teach them to *seek* the Lord's will in everything (Psalm 37:5).
- Encourage them to be *dependent* upon the Lord for every aspect of their lives (Psalm 37:23; Prov. 3:5, 6).
- Help them to find their God-given *gifts* and then develop them.

CLOSING THE GAP ON LESSON 4

In Your Group:

1. What can we do to keep promises at home or in our relationships?
2. Ask this: who may be the person in my relationships or home who needs my kind attention now? *(Each individual names one person).*
3. What can I do to express kindness to the person I named above?
4. Lord willing, six months from now, my life will reflect this promise. Date: ______________

Personal Evaluation on Your Own

On a scale of 1-10 (1 being "I totally disagree" and 10 being "I totally agree), rate yourself in the following areas:

1. I am a servant to my relationships. ___________
2. When I make a promise to the people in my life, they know I will always keep it. ___________
3. I recognize personal & emotional wounds suffered in the past & have learned how to compensate for them. ______
4. I am modeling absolute dependence on the Lord for every detail of my life. ___________
5. When it comes to the ultimate purpose in life and each of my relationships, they understand how I feel about a connection with Christ and share that core value with me.

CHAPTER 5

A Disciple and Their Church

A DISCIPLE IS COMMITTED TO SUPPORTING THE MISSION OF THEIR CHURCH BY HONORING AND PRAYING FOR THEIR PASTOR AND BY ACTIVELY GIVING OF THEIR TIME AND RESOURCES TO THE CHURCH

In *The Master Plan of Evangelism,* Robert Coleman, Director of Trinity Evangelical Divinity's School of World Missions and Evangelism, provides a purpose statement for evangelism. He affirms that Jesus' ministry had a clear objective. He intended to *save out of the world* a people for Himself and to build a church of the Spirit which would never perish.[15]

Jesus' intention was to evangelize, make disciples, and integrate them into a dynamic church community. All true believers are disciples, and the Christian life is about daily living out this aspect of Jesus' teaching. Salvation was not only to bring people

[15] Robert E. Coleman, *The Master Plan of Evangelism* (Old Tappan: Revell, 1964), 17.

into the Kingdom but, ideally, to introduce individuals into the group discipleship process.[16]

Therefore, with all of the elements of discipleship, i.e., Prayer to the Father, Study of the Word, Fellowship with believers and Evangelistic witness, linked together, the Body of Christ will be divinely established to play an important role of Evangelism in preparation for existence in God's eternal kingdom. Without the Church doing what I would call "The Big Four," we have no life. All four of these elements should happen in the Church. The apostle Paul tells us what my pastor, Dr. Lea called the 20/20 vision in the Book of Acts Chapter 20:20,

> *And when they came to him, he said to them: "You yourselves know how I lived among you the whole time from the first day that I set foot in Asia, serving the Lord with all humility and with tears and with trials that happened to me through the plots of the Jews; how I did not shrink from declaring to you anything that was profitable, and teaching you in public and from house to house, testifying both to Jews and to Greeks of repentance toward God and of faith in our Lord Jesus Christ. (Acts 20:18-21)*

These verses emphasize teaching, which would indicate a public setting, like churches or in house gatherings. The church must have community support for its meetings other than those in which people participate on Sunday mornings. These house meetings involve praying, sharing God's Word, fellowshipping over food, praying for each other, and inviting neighbors to join.

---

[16] Coleman, 52.

Often, people will attend a meeting in someone's house before they actually decide to attend a church. The essentials of supporting the mission of the church obviously require people to do all four of these things, i.e., pray for one another, share the word with one another, fellowship around food with each other, and invite people to their homes, and eventually to their churches. This is what makes what I call a significant and very participatory church for its believers.

One day, Dr. Lea said that all the church members were to see themselves as an extension of the pulpit. Contrary to his assertion, I did not see myself as a minister, or call myself a minister, or see myself as an extension of the pulpit in any context. Earnestly, Dr. Lea was calling all of us as congregant ministers, extensions of the pulpit, i.e., the "Church." His premises were based on the body of believers as mentioned in Ephesians being equipped to do the work of the ministry. So many capacities of the church require every member to do their part.

> *And he gave the apostles, the prophets, the evangelists, the shepherds and teachers, to equip the saints for the work of ministry, for building up the body of Christ. (Eph. 4:11–12)*

This was a very profound and fundamental statement of how the church should work. I had not heard this context of the scripture from any pastor that I grew up with, in my Presbyterian faith, or any Sunday sermon, or in any Bible study that I had known. I suddenly took these words to heart and did so very seriously. That was another *180-degree turning point* for me.

Up to this point, I did not see myself as an extension of the pulpit as Dr. Lea intimated, but I was now intrigued by the possibility. This was not far from what my Grandma saw in me, not as only a member sitting with my mind open to be fed the Word of God but as an extension of what was happening in the ministry and the local church. Like most churchgoers, I only saw myself as a member sitting there with my mind wide open to receive. Dr. Ken Mayton, former director of the D.Min. Program at ORU seminary, used to say that most people are like this description of the average churchgoer.

> *"Your head is empty. Your head is hollow, look out, look out, there's more to follow. Over the teeth, over the gums, look out stomach, here it comes."*

It is very profound that most of the time, believers do not see themselves as extensions or, more so, as disciples of Jesus Christ. As Dr. Charles Snow had mentioned earlier, it is the Church's purpose to complete the model that Jesus left in Matthew 28, the church is supposed to infiltrate the world and make disciples.

Dr. Snow's definition of discipleship of the "loyal, learning followers of Jesus Christ," forms the theology that I have adopted and is the purpose of this treatise that is in your hands. All churches need discipleship in their congregation. It also means that individuals really are an extension of the pastoral pulpit of the church. Their heads are not so empty that they cannot understand what's going on, or their stomachs are not so empty that they should be more than satisfied with the word of God that tells them to be active in the body.

Overall, people know that the Word encourages them to want to do "The Big Four" work of discipleship. No pastor should do it alone, but that was how I grew up; it was the pastor's job to pray for everyone, visit every sick person, speak and preach every Sunday and Wednesday, and attend special events. They were also required to bury the dead and christen the babies.

Since then, I have learned that the congregants are extensions of the pulpit. This was a phenomenon that my pastor presented, that every congregation should have and should do. The Word tells us to know those that labor among you. What kind of labor? It would have to be the work of the Ministry related in Ephesians Chapter 4.

> *(In saying, "He ascended," what does it mean but that he had also descended into the lower regions, the earth? He who descended is the one who also ascended far above all the heavens, that he might fill all things.) And he gave the apostles, the prophets, the evangelists, the shepherds and teachers, to equip the saints for the work of ministry, for building up the body of Christ, until we all attain to the unity of the faith and of the knowledge of the Son of God, to mature manhood, to the measure of the stature of the fullness of Christ, so that we may no longer be children, tossed to and fro by the waves and carried about by every wind of doctrine, by human cunning, by craftiness in deceitful schemes. Rather, speaking the truth in love, we are to grow up in every way into him who is the head, into Christ, from whom the whole body, joined and held together by every joint with which it is equipped, when each part is working properly, makes the body grow so that it builds itself up in love. (Eph. 4:9–16)*

Paul speaks of God's grace given in a variety of expressions to each one of us ("all believers" as "we" and "us" elsewhere in the letter). He is not restricting the scope of what he says to the ministers in v. 11. This leads him to a description of Christ as the giver of all such graces.[17]

[17] D. A Carson et al., *Ephesians*, ed., New Bible Commentary: 21st Century Edition. Accordance electronic ed. (Downers Grove: InterVarsity Press, 1994), 1236.

Lesson for Chapter 5

A Disciple and Their Church

A DISCIPLE IS COMMITTED TO SUPPORTING THE MISSION OF THEIR CHURCH BY HONORING AND PRAYING FOR THEIR PASTOR AND BY ACTIVELY GIVING THEIR TIME AND RESOURCES TO THE CHURCH.

CORE ISSUE: HONOR

KEY PASSAGE:

We ask you, brothers, to respect those who labor among you and are over you in the Lord and admonish you, and to esteem them very highly in love because of their work. Be at peace among yourselves. (1 Thess. 5:12-13)

Obey your leaders and submit to them, for they are keeping watch over your souls, as those who will have to give an account. Let them do this with joy and not with groaning, for that would be of no advantage to you. (Heb. 13:17)

WARM-UP DISCUSSION:

Everyone would like to have more money and time. We dream of winning a multimillion-dollar lotto jackpot, being independently wealthy, or gaining extra vacation time. If you were given $1,000,000 and could spend it and not use it to pay bills, how would you spend it? How do you think this would change you?

BACKGROUND

It is amazing how we differ in opinions. In the words above, we just observed our differences when it comes to money and time. Today's session will address differences of a more profound nature. Jesus used a parable to lead his hearers into new insights about life. We need to keep in mind that a biblical parable is not only intended to teach a principle with a deeper meaning but also to sort out the mixed motives of the hearers. The parable today will help us to see that there are differing responses to the Word of God.

LET'S READ: Mark 4:1-20

Again he began to teach beside the sea. And a very large crowd gathered about him, so that he got into a boat and sat in it on the sea, and the whole crowd was beside the sea on the land. And he was teaching them many things in parables, and in his teaching, he said to them: "Listen! Behold, a sower went out to sow. And as he sowed, some seed fell along the path, and the birds came and devoured it.

Other seed fell on rocky ground, where it did not have much soil, and immediately it sprang up, since it had no depth of soil. And when the sun rose, it was scorched, and since it had no root, it withered away. Other seed fell among thorns, and the thorns grew up and choked it, and it yielded no grain. And other seeds fell into good soil and produced grain, growing up and increasing and yielding thirtyfold and sixtyfold and a hundredfold." And he said, "He who has ears to hear, let him hear."

And when he was alone, those around him with the twelve asked him about the parables. And he said to them, "To you has been given the secret of the kingdom of God, but for those outside everything is in parables, so that 'they may indeed see but not perceive, and may indeed hear but not understand, lest they should turn and be forgiven.' And he said to them, "Do you not understand this parable? How then will you understand all the parables?

The sower sows the word. And these are the ones along the path, where the word is sown: when they hear, Satan immediately comes and takes away the word that is sown in them. And these are the ones sown on rocky ground: the ones who, when they hear the word, immediately receive it with joy. And they have no root in themselves but endure for a while; then, when tribulation or persecution arises on account of the word, immediately they fall away. And others are the ones sown among thorns. They are those who hear the word, but the cares of the world and the deceitfulness of riches and the desires for other things enter in and choke the word, and it proves unfruitful. But those that were sown on the good soil are the ones who hear the word and accept it and bear fruit, thirtyfold and sixtyfold and a hundredfold."

QUESTIONS FOR REFLECTION:

1. In churches today, people sing the same songs and hear the same messages, yet we all interpret and apply the message differently. How do we explain this?
2. When this farmer sows broadly, where does the seed land?
3. What is the seed in this parable?
4. In what ways are the soils a picture of our hearts?
5. Why doesn't the seed germinate equally well in each of the soils?
6. What are the examples of thorns in our own experience?

CONSIDER THIS:

The vast majority of our pastors feel beat up, overworked, and disrespected. The result is a shepherd who is disheartened, discouraged, and worn out, often questioning his own worth and call to the ministry. John tells us that the Father honors the one who serves Him. The pastor has honored God by being obedient to His call and by giving his life in service to the Lord. Therefore, if we choose not to honor the pastor, we are giving dishonor to the one God is honoring.

CRITICAL STEPS:

RESPECT

1. See your pastor as God's leader to you.
2. Think the best of your pastor. (Give your pastor the benefit of the doubt.)
3. Speak well of your pastor.
4. Help stop any gossip or criticism of your pastor.
5. Guard your pastor's time with the family by not unnecessarily calling them at home.

PRAYER

1. Cover your pastor's ministry, vision, wisdom, and health.
2. Ask for favor with the congregation and among your pastor's colleagues.
3. Pray for your pastor's family members that they will have health, unity, joy, and their needs met.
4. Pray positive Scripture into your pastor's life and ministry.

ASSISTANCE:

Help share your pastor's load in areas where this is possible;

1. Researching, gathering, and evaluating information.
2. Running errands.
3. Doing visitation.

4. Counseling.
5. Planning, brainstorming, being a sounding board.
6. Provide proper and adequate compensation from the church budget.

ENCOURAGE

1. Show appreciation for messages and hard work.
2. Compliment, where appropriate, your pastor's children and spouse.
3. Write notes of appreciation - they can be observed later when your pastor is in need of some encouragement.
4. Pray often on your pastor's behalf and directly ask how you can better pray for your pastor.
5. Inquire later about the status of prayer requests your pastor has given.
6. Invite the family to dinner.
7. Help the church give a useful gift at Christmas, birthday, anniversary, or a "thank-you" for many years of service.

PERSONAL EVALUATION *(On Your Own)*

1. I honor and respect my pastor.
2. I communicate this respect to my pastor.
3. I positively pray for my pastor.
4. I ask my pastor in what areas help is needed.
5. How do we know what kind of soil we are? What kind of soil would you like to be? Explain?

PERSONAL EVALUATION *(In the Group)*

1. How can this group help me turn poor soil into good soil?
2. What might be a thorn in my life that is choking the growth of God's Word?
3. How do you feel when criticized for the way you're doing something into which you have poured your heart? Discuss the feelings that might occur when the same thing is done to your pastor.
4. How can you stop someone who wants to gossip, run down the pastor, or question the pastor's ways?
5. How can you more effectively honor your pastor? What are some ways in which you can do this or have done it? Please share with the group.
6. What would be the best way to address a problem you see with your pastor? Discuss options.

CLOSING THE GAP ON LESSON 5

Setting a Prayerful Horizon:

1. I commit to pray this week for each of these brothers to develop good soil.
2. Lord willing, six months from now, my life will reflect this promise in these ways:

ACCOUNTABILITY COMMITMENT:

Who:____

When: ____

CHAPTER 6

A Disciple and Their Neighbors

A DISCIPLE IS COMMITTED TO REACHING BEYOND ANY CULTURAL, ECONOMIC, RACIAL, GENDER, OR DENOMINATIONAL BARRIER TO DEMONSTRATE THE POWER OF BIBLICAL UNITY.

In the movie "Gone Baby Gone," the opening dialogue articulates a widely held definition of culture.

> *I have always believed it was the things you don't choose that make you who you are, your city, your neighborhood, your family. People take pride in these things as if it were something they had accomplished, the bodies around their souls, the cities wrapped around those. It helps to know where people started.*[18]

[18] "*Gone Baby Gone*". A 2007 movie directed by Ben Affleck. Screenplay by Ben Affleck and Aaron Stockard. Based on the book *Gone Baby Gone* by Dennis Lehane. (William Morrow & Co. 1998)

Culture, like described above, is background, traditions, and customs that can only be articulated in our own language, our own understanding.

Culture really does start where we come from. I grew up a son of Afro-American parents; my father was originally from rural Charlotte, North Carolina, and my mother was originally from a small rural town in Marietta, Georgia. Both were products of post-slavery African and Native American heritage who lived in the southeastern United States. Rather than recounting the entire history of the descendants of ex-slaves, I find that the word "ex-slave" alone encapsulates the essence of my cultural background. It not only connects me to my ancestors' struggles but also highlights the resilience and traditions that have shaped my family's values and my own sense of identity.

I lived in a world with two realities. The first was the life that my parents grew up in and eventually out of, becoming a middle-class, black family, very representative of the 60s and 70s in America. The other representation was one that reminded us of how challenging, as a minority, life would be and what we needed for success in our lives going forward. My mother believed that education, especially for Afro-Americans, would be the key to all our successes. She would always say, "You can go anywhere and be or do anything you want." This principle still guides my life and my upcoming book project, "Jump Culture for God's Sake." It does not suggest abandoning one's past; rather, a cultural jump which involves embracing new perspectives. Since culture is deeply rooted in our history and identity, such a shift requires a fundamental change in how we view life.

The two Greek words for time are *Kairos* and *Kronos*. The importance of *Kairos* is that it is God's appointed time for events to take place specifically for his purposes to be achieved. *Kronos* is clock time, or the space of time that God created, specifically for men to occupy until Jesus comes again. I have been a Star Trek fan ("Trekkie") for most of my life. I see God as a jumper of culture through what is called in *Star Trek,* "The Space-Time Continuum," similar to God's connections of culture that can only be described by His theophanies (appearances), to the inhabitants of His creation. We can call it "God's Space-Time Continuum," reiterating that from Genesis 1:1 to its culmination in Revelation 22:21, the biblical text brings the ultimate cultural jump of a people to live and enjoy eternity with him. We see in the book of Revelation, Chapter 7:9-10.

> *After this I looked, and behold, a great multitude that no one could number, from every nation, from all tribes and peoples and languages, standing before the throne and before the Lamb, clothed in white robes, with palm branches in their hands, and crying out with a loud voice, "Salvation belongs to our God who sits on the throne, and to the Lamb!" (Rev. 7:9–10)*

Since the time I graduated with my D.Min. from ORU in 1997, Addie and I began to discuss where we had been and where we were going. I have spent most of my life exploring other nations and other people groups, both in the context of a student, and a professor with students from all over the world. I have basically done this while teaching, which has become my main tool to familiarize myself with others, and jump culture in the classroom.

I have endeavored to graciously accept the journey that will take me/us to different cultures. I will always find myself operating to make disciples, as it has become the tool by which the Holy Spirit works through me as Jesus prophesied in Matthew:

> *And Jesus came and said to them, "All authority in heaven and on earth has been given to me. Go therefore and make disciples of all nations, baptizing them in the name of the Father and of the Son and of the Holy Spirit, teaching them to observe all that I have commanded you. And behold, I am with you always, to the end of the age. (Matt. 28:18-20)*

We moved into a new neighborhood in the Fall of 2020. As a result of that we encountered our new neighbors. It is amazing that when you don't know the people that live around you, you have two opportunities. Get to know them or isolate yourself to not know them.

According to the Bible, particularly in Jesus' Parable of the Good Samaritan (Luke 10:25-37), your neighbor is

anyone in need, regardless of race, religion, or social status. It extends beyond proximity to include even enemies, requiring proactive love, mercy, and compassion for anyone God places in your path.

A neighbor is defined by their need and your ability to help, not just by geographical proximity. The "Good Samaritan" is an excellent illustration made by Jesus in Luke 10:25-37. A neighbor is the person who shows mercy, breaking down cultural or personal barriers.

And behold, a lawyer stood up to put him to the test, saying, "Teacher, what shall I do to inherit eternal life?" He said to him, "What is written in the Law? How do you read it?" And he answered, "You shall love the Lord your God with all your heart and with all your soul and with all your strength and with all your mind, and your neighbor as yourself." And he said to him, "You have answered correctly; do this, and you will live."

But he, (a lawyer) desiring to justify himself, said to Jesus, "And who is my neighbor?" Jesus replied, "A man was going down from Jerusalem to Jericho, and he fell among robbers, who stripped him and beat him and departed, leaving him half dead. Now by chance a priest was going down that road, and when he saw him he passed by on the other side. So likewise a Levite, when he came to the place and saw him, passed by on the other side.

But a Samaritan, as he journeyed, came to where he was, and when he saw him, he had compassion. He went to him and bound up his wounds, pouring on oil and wine. Then he set him on his own animal and brought him to an inn and took care of him. And the next day he took out two denarii and gave them to the innkeeper, saying, 'Take care of him, and whatever more you spend, I will repay you when I come back.' Which of these three, do you think, proved to be a neighbor to the man who fell among the robbers?" He said, "The one who showed him mercy." And Jesus said to him, "You go, and do likewise." (Luke 10:25–37)

I believe this passage of scripture is a turning point in the gospel. The Jews were bound up by their culture. I had one prophet share that; Culture can sometimes be stronger than the anointing of God. The concept of the *"Jump Culture"* Phenomenon is in essence *"Universal Love,"* the command "Love your neighbor as yourself" (Matthew 22:39) implies that every person you encounter is your neighbor. Active compassion is being a neighbor and involves taking action to meet the needs of others. In short, your neighbor is anyone you have the opportunity to show God's love to, regardless of who they are.

I have traveled to several countries in the world , and there are a few things that I have always come to consider doing while I'm there. The major issue is to identify what are the aspects of culture; what the culture likes to do socially, how the culture prepares and eats their food, and most importantly how the culture dresses. I remember when I went to India, which was my first journey outside of America and my home.

While I was there, I wore an Indian shirt called a kurta and one young man actually said, *"you look very Indian."* That made me feel so much a part of that culture. Since then, wherever I have gone, I want to know what it is that the culture does. This *"Jump Culture"* phenomenon is important for all of us today and especially in this time. One of my professors, Dr. Trever Grizzle spoke and wrote about culture in one of his works, *Church Aflame: An Exposition of Acts 1-12.* [19]

In a class that I attended Dr. Grizzle said that there are three incidents in the Bible where culture was so imperative that God had to intervene to help people be what he wanted them to be instead of what they wanted themselves to be. Dr. Grizzle touches on two of those incidents in *Church Aflame*. The first

[19] Dr. Trevor Grizzle, *Church Aflame, An Exposition of Acts 1-12*

incident is in Genesis chapter 11 where we find after the flood people were traveling along the plain of Shinar. Men wanted to build a tower to heaven and supposedly to reach God. The efforts were not in essence to communicate with God, but the belief is that they wanted to be where God was, maybe even to take over.

> *Now the whole earth had one language and the same words. And as people migrated from the east, they found a plain in the land of Shinar and settled there. And they said to one another, "Come, let us make bricks, and burn them thoroughly." And they had brick for stone, and bitumen for mortar. Then they said, "Come, let us build ourselves a city and a tower with its top in the heavens, and let us make a name for ourselves, lest we be dispersed over the face of the whole earth." And the Lord came down to see the city and the tower, which the children of man had built. And the Lord said, "Behold, they are one people, and they have all one language, and this is only the beginning of what they will do. And nothing that they propose to do will now be impossible for them. Come, let us go down and there confuse their language, so that they may not understand one another's speech." So the Lord dispersed them from there over the face of all the earth, and they left off building the city. Therefore its name was called Babel, because there the Lord confused the language of all the earth. And from there the Lord dispersed them over the face of all the earth. (Genesis 11:1–9)*

Genesis 11:1–9 reveals The Tower of Babel or *"Forced Homogeneity"*[20] as a cultural state of forced Monoculture Unity. The entire human race spoke one language and shared a single purpose (Gen 11:1). Pride-driven urbanization and technology says, *"let us make bricks," "build a city," "make a name for ourselves."* This was not God's idea of a neighbor. This culture was based on self-exaltation rather than divine command to fill the earth. God saw this, and, as a judgment on their pride and disobedience to fill the earth (Gen 9:1), He "confused their language" to force them to disperse. This forced scattering, produced distinct nations and languages. The cultural "divide" was a necessary, protective act of grace to prevent humanity from fully consolidating in rebellion.

The second incident that Dr. Grizzle points out is what he calls a reversal of Genesis 11. This happens in the book of act chapter 2 with the baptism of the Holy Spirit. In this incident, there were people gathered in Jerusalem to celebrate the feasts from every nation, kindred and tongue. It lists who they were and where they are from.

> *When the day of Pentecost arrived, they were all together in one place. And suddenly there came from heaven a sound like a mighty rushing wind, and it filled the entire house where they were sitting. And divided tongues as of fire appeared to them and rested on each one of them. And they were all filled with the Holy Spirit and began to speak in other tongues as the Spirit gave them utterance.*
>
> *Now there were dwelling in Jerusalem Jews, devout men from every nation under heaven. And at this sound the*

[20] https://share.google/aimode/4ugxVRssx8gRyZ9UC

multitude came together, and they were bewildered, because each one was hearing them speak in his own language. And they were amazed and astonished, saying, "Are not all these who are speaking Galileans?

And how is it that we hear each of us in his own native language? Parthians and Medes and Elamites and residents of Mesopotamia, Judea and Cappadocia, Pontus and Asia, Phrygia and Pamphylia, Egypt and the parts of Libya belonging to Cyrene, and visitors from Rome, both Jews and proselytes, Cretans and Arabians—we hear them telling in our own tongues the mighty works of God." And all were amazed and perplexed, saying to one another, "What does this mean?" (Acts 2:1–12)

Acts 2:1–13 describes Pentecost, and was *"Redeemed Diversity."* The cultural state was Multicultural Inclusion/ Diverse Unity. This event is often seen as the reversal of Babel, not by destroying diversity, but by redeeming it. It is also a cultural expression: The disciples were enabled to speak in different languages, "as the Spirit gave them utterance" (Acts 2:4). The crowd included people from "every nation under heaven" (Parthians, Medes, Romans, etc.). The Holy Spirit did not erase the languages of the crowd to create one language, but enabled the gospel to be understood *in* their native, diverse languages.[21] The outcome was a *"multicultural insurrection"* against the monoculture of the Roman world, bringing various cultures under the lordship of Jesus while retaining their unique identities.

[21] https://share.google/aimode/4ugxVRssx8gRyZ9UC

The third incident in Revelation 7:9–17, is the New Jerusalem or "*Final Harmony.*" The cultural state or eternal, harmonious unity is a *"great multitude that no one could count."* They gathered before the throne. The multitude comes from "every nation, tribe, people and language" (Rev 7:9). Unlike Babel, where God separates people, or Pentecost, where God breaks communication barriers, Revelation depicts God gathering everyone *together*. Cultural diversity is not eliminated in heaven, but redeemed and celebrated. People retain their ethnic/cultural identity, i.e., *"every tribe and tongue,"* but are united in worshiping the Lamb.[22]

We in the church concentrate on the baptism of the Holy Spirit, but God also wants a *"Jump Culture"* phenomenon. The people said; "*And how is it that we hear each of us in his own native language?*" This was a phenomenon of the Holy Spirit's ability to make us hear people as they spoke in their own language.

The third *"Jump Culture"* phenomenon occurs in the book of revelation chapter 7:9f. There is around the throne, a multitude that no one could number from every nation, kindred and tongue. How is this even possible? The fact that God has now finally brought men back to worship with him was a *"Jump Culture"* phenomenal event. It seems to me that God loves diversity and in that diverse concept, he does not care that we were different. He just wants us to enjoy each other's company. In other words, with our differences and enjoying each other, we are literally neighbors.

I have come to know several of my neighbors since we moved into our new neighborhood. I think it's important that

---

[22] https://share.google/aimode/4ugxVRssx8gRyZ9UC

we, regardless of our race, nature, nationality, and culture, not only get out, walk around, but also talk to our neighbors. Get to know them and have fellowship with them, maybe even to share a meal, or customs that we have that they would like. In essence, the whole purpose of loving your neighbor is to be a carrier and a sharer of the gospel of Jesus Christ. You never know who will come to the knowledge of the possibility of spending eternity together, get saved and stand before God with you in His heavenly abode.

My southern African-American life and food, and my wife's East Indian nature and cuisine, are totally different, but we enjoy each other's cuisine and also certain aspects of each other's culture. Is this what it is going to be like in heaven when we have the feast? OK, let's wait and see what we get, but consider that we only get there through making Jesus Christ Lord of our lives. Only then we will all be truly eternal neighbors. I think God is waiting for us to accept the fact that we will all be different despite our race, nature, kindred and tongue. He wants us all to be neighbors.

These three incidents in the Bible point out that true kingdom fellowship must model mutual respect and love, and not the idea that we own or can conquer any other culture outside of ourselves. Heaven will be a place where we mingle and communicate with each other. Just imagine what it really means to start seeing your neighbor as you see yourself.

Lesson for Chapter 6

A Disciple and Their Neighbors

A DISCIPLE OF JESUS CHRIST IS COMMITTED TO REACHING BEYOND ANY CULTURAL, ECONOMIC, RACIAL, GENDER, OR DENOMINATIONAL BARRIER TO DEMONSTRATE THE POWER OF BIBLICAL UNITY.

CORE ISSUE: UNITY

KEY PASSAGE:

I do not ask for these only, but also for those who will believe in me through their word, that they may all be one, just as you, Father, are in me, and I in you, that they also may be in us, so that the world may believe that you have sent me. The glory that you have given me I have given to them, that they may be one even as we are one, I in them and you in me, that they may become perfectly one, so that the world may know that you sent me and loved them even as you loved me. (John 17:20-23)

WARM-UP DISCUSSION:

We live in communities today where we hardly know our neighbors. In the world that you live in, who are your neighbors? Our world seems impersonal because of our pace of life, and in a sense, we are afraid to get involved in the lives of the people around us. Why is that? What qualities do you look for in a good friend or a neighbor?

BACKGROUND:

A neighbor is commonly thought to be the person next door or someone who lives in a location near you. In the time of the New Testament, however, ***neighbor*** commonly meant "one living in the same land." In essence, a neighbor in that context might have included several villages or towns. The Jews split hairs over this question and were excluded from their "neighbors," Gentiles and especially Samaritans. So, here was their loophole. A neighbor is a nigh dweller to one, but the Jews made racial exceptions as many, alas, do today.

LET'S READ: Luke 10:25-37

And behold, a lawyer stood up to put him to the test, saying, "Teacher, what shall I do to inherit eternal life?" He said to him, "What is written in the Law? How do you read it?" And he answered, "You shall love the Lord your God with all your heart and with all your soul and with all your strength and with all your mind, and your neighbor as yourself." And he said to him, "You have answered correctly; do this, and you will live."

But he, desiring to justify himself, said to Jesus, "And who is my neighbor?" Jesus replied, "A man was going down from Jerusalem to Jericho, and he fell among robbers, who stripped him and beat him and departed, leaving him half dead. Now by chance a priest was going down that road, and when he saw him, he passed by on the other side. So likewise, a Levite, when he came to the place and saw him, passed by on the other side.

But a Samaritan, as he journeyed, came to where he was, and when he saw him, he had compassion. He went to him and bound up his wounds, pouring on oil and wine. Then he set him on his own animal and brought him to an inn and took care of him. And the next day he took out two denarii and gave them to the innkeeper, saying, 'Take care of him, and whatever more you spend, I will repay you when I come back.' Which of these three, do you think, proved to be a neighbor to the man who fell among the robbers?" He said, "The one who showed him mercy." And Jesus said to him, "You go, and do likewise." (Luke 10:25–37)

When we moved into our new neighborhood about three years ago, we were one of the first three houses. In our previous home we owned, we lived there for over 20 years. We literally knew all the houses around us and most of the neighbors in our neighborhood. We had fellowship with a few of them, especially those who were believers. Mike and Andrea were Christian friends living directly across the street. As a matter of fact, their daughter had been a babysitter a few times for her kids growing up. Mike was and is my insurance broker keeping me ahead of my insurance needs. Right before I retired Mike gave me advice to start drawing my SSI at 67. I intended to wait till I was 70 years old.

> *"Why wait, because it's your money and it is available now. A lot of people wait because they think they will get an increase at the age of 70, but it would not be that much and if you got it now, you could get out a lot of your debts."*

That was good neighborly advice given to me. Mike still helps me with my SSI insurance and supplements. I was Mike's spiritual advisor to many of the issues that he was going through. We have kept this relationship going over many years, and I believe it an example of what loving your neighbors can produce.

We moved into our new neighborhood in the fall of 2020. We know a few of the neighbors right around us, but we don't really know a lot of the people in the neighborhood. As long as I don't know who my neighbor is, does that let me off the hook? Do I have to get to know them, and what is my responsibility to those around me?

QUESTIONS FOR REFLECTION:

Agree/disagree, and explain your answer:

1. As long as I don't know who my neighbor is, I have no responsibility to them.
2. What did the first two men who encountered this man have in common? Why did they not stop and help him? What motivated the Samaritan to stop and help? What builds compassion in a life?

3. If this scene was on the freeways of your city, and like what happened in Jericho, what might keep you from stopping? Under what conditions would you have stopped to help?
4. What does it mean to be a neighbor, according to Jesus?

CRITICAL STEPS
EIGHT PRINCIPLES OF RECONCILIATION:*

PRINCIPLE 1: Commitment to Relationship

Reconciliation is built upon the foundation of committed relationships.

But Ruth said, 'Do not urge me to leave you or to return from following you. For where you go, I will go, and where you lodge. I will lodge. Your people shall be my people, and your God my God.' (Ruth 1:16)

Key Issues Regarding Relationship:

- Conflict
- Resolution

PRINCIPLE 2: Intentionality

Intentionality is the purposeful, positive and planned activity that facilitates reconciliation.

For he himself is our peace, who has made us both one and has broken down in his flesh the dividing wall of hostility by abolishing the law of commandments expressed in ordinances, that he might create in himself one new man in place of the two, so making peace. (Eph. 2:14-15)

Key Issue Regarding Intentionality: Perseverance

PRINCIPLE 3: Sincerity

Sincerity is the willingness to be vulnerable, including the self-disclosure of feelings, attitudes, differences and perceptions, with the goals of resolution and trust.

No longer do I call you servants, for the servant does not know what his master is doing; but I have called you friends, for all that I have heard from my Father I have made known to you. (John 15:15)

Key Issues Regarding Sincerity:

- Trust
- Transparency

PRINCIPLE 4: Sensitivity

Sensitivity is the intentional acquisition of knowledge in order to relate empathetically to a person of a different race, culture, or denomination.

Rather, speaking the truth in love, we are to grow up in every way into him who is the head, into Christ, from whom the whole body, joined and held together by every joint with which it is equipped, when each part is working properly, makes the body grow so that it builds itself up in love. (Eph. 4:15-16)

Key Issues Regarding Sensitivity:

- Knowledge
- Truth Seeking

PRINCIPLE 5: Interdependence

Interdependence recognizes our differences but realizes that we each offer something that the other person needs, resulting in equality in the relationship.

For if the readiness is there, it is acceptable according to what a person has, not according to what he does not have. For I do not mean that others should be eased, and you burdened, but that as a matter of fairness your abundance at the present time should supply their need, so that their abundance may supply your need, that there may be fairness. (2Cor. 8:12-14)

Key Issue Regarding Interdependence: Equality

PRINCIPLE 6: Sacrifice

Sacrifice is the willingness to relinquish an established status of position to genuinely adopt a lesser position in order to facilitate a cross-cultural relationship.

Do nothing from selfish ambition or conceit, but in humility count others more significant than yourselves. Let each of you look not only to his own interests, but also to the interests of others. (Phil. 2:3-4)

Key Issue Regarding Sacrifice: Cost

PRINCIPLE 7: Empowerment

Empowerment is the use of repentance and forgiveness to create complete freedom in a cross-cultural relationship.

For you know the grace of our Lord Jesus Christ, that though he was rich, yet for your sake he became poor, so that you by his poverty might become rich. (2 Cor. 8:9)

Key Issues Regarding Empowerment:

- Repentance
- Forgiveness

PRINCIPLE 8: Calling

We are all called to be involved in the ministry of reconciliation, but some are gifted with a special call to be reconcilers.

Therefore, if anyone is in Christ, he is a new creation. The old has passed away; behold, the new has come. All this is from God, who through Christ reconciled us to himself and gave us the ministry of reconciliation; that is, in Christ God was reconciling the world to himself, not counting their trespasses against them, and entrusting to us the message of reconciliation. Therefore, we are ambassadors for Christ, God making his appeal through us. We implore you on behalf of Christ, be reconciled to God. For our sake he made him to be sin who knew no sin, so that in him we might become the righteousness of God. (2 Cor. 5:17-21)

PERSONAL EVALUATION

On a scale of 1-10 (1 being "I totally disagree" and 10 being "I totally agree), rate yourself in the following areas:

1. I am reaching beyond racial and cultural barriers. _____
2. I am reaching beyond denominational barriers. _____
3. I am demonstrating the power of biblical unity. _____

IN THE GROUP

1. As you think about reaching across denominational, culture or racial barriers, what are your biggest concerns?
2. How can you take the first step to establish relationships with brothers of different denominational or ethnic backgrounds?

**Taken from Breaking Down the Walls—A Model of Reconciliation in an Age of Racial Strife, by Raleigh Washington and Glen Kehrein. © 1993, Raleigh Washington and Glen Kehrein, Moody Press. Used by Permission.*

CHAPTER 7

Disciples and Their World

DISCIPLES ARE COMMITTED TO INFLUENCING THEIR WORLD, BEING OBEDIENT TO THE GREAT COMMANDMENT (MARK 12:30-31) AND THE GREAT COMMISSION (MATT. 28:19-20)

It was mission week at COTR in Rockwall, Texas. The appeal to go on missions excited me as I listened to the speaker from India. He was a businessman, named Dr. P.J. Titus, who had come to America and made his living making the American dollar. He decided to go back to India and plant a Bible school and was encouraged when Dr. Lea agreed to help him in this project to plant the new Church on the Rock Bible College (COTR-BC) in Visakhapatnam, in the state of Andhra Pradesh. The school would be affiliated with Oral Roberts University (ORU) as Dr. Lea was the Associate Dean of the Seminary, and would help students in India achieve credit for lessons taught. He insisted that I had to achieve my Doctor of Ministry Degree (D.Min.) to be qualified to teach in the school in India.

The design was to evangelize north India, an under-evangelized region of the country. To understand Dr. Titus' desire, it must be understood that north India was populated by Muslims and Sikhs. Dr. Titus had developed an evangelistic schema to educate and train evangelists to infiltrate that area of India.

I became excited about the possibility of fulfilling the 1982 prophecy that I would go around the world teaching and sharing. I desired from that moment hearing Dr. Titus to go to India and wherever the Lord would send me. In the ensuing months, as Dr. Lea's vision became more familiar, the Mission director Dr. David Shibley and a team that included me, traveled to India in 1988 to start the school. I knew this would open the opportunity for me to go to India as a missionary/teacher and work in that Bible school.

The missions Director, Dr. David Shibley, and Dr. Lea, were excited to realize that my wife, Adeline, was from India, which would be a real plus. I had also become acquainted with several Indian people in our church. Dr. Titus's nephew, Mathew Thomas, was to attend ORU at the same time and get his degree as well, and he eventually became the director of COTR-BC. There was also Rita Mellon, a friend of my wife Addie from India, who had originally introduced me to Addie. These all joined my cell fellowship group when I became an expansion leader in the Singles Cell Group Ministry at COTR, multiplying out of my friend Jim Schwartz's group. I eventually became an associate Pastor at COTR.

Since then, the immersion, education, and otherworldly experiences that I received while attending and working at ORU have taken me to foreign cities in Mexico, India, Russia,

Great Britain and the Fiji Isles. Additionally, I have gone to several cities throughout the United States. Amazingly, I have taught students from over 150 different nations as Director of the D.Min. Degree Program for 5 years and a professor at ORU for the past 30 years.

A great deal has happened since that little fellowship group in Rockwall, Texas. God has sent me around the world to teach, preach, and reach a world in desperate need of Jesus Christ. It has been an awesome journey and growth experience going into another person's world. Everyone should seize the opportunity to explore a world outside of their own domain.

The mandate or commandments from Jesus in Mark 16 and Matthew 28 are pretty emphatic. I pray the impact will begin to affect you as it has done to me. Ask yourself, "What does discipleship look like for me?"

I am proposing that the need of individuals in the world will pull some and catapult them down the road to discipleship success, which can only happen when they practice the "Big Four" of Prayer to the Father, Word of God study, Fellowship with believers and a call to Evangelism.

As you investigate the mandate that God has given to us all, it will become revelatory, and ultimately encourage you to aid in ushering in the kingdom of God. I really believe the return of Jesus Christ is precipitated by our obedience to participate in the great commission and great commandment.

The Word of God has been presented to us with a mighty mandate to make disciples of all nations. The word in Greek is *(ethnos)* and in Hebrew *(goyim), which means people from every walk of life.* We have been called, and I pray that our obedience would be like that of God's servant Abraham, who became the father of many nations of people.

Those who choose to serve the Father God will come to an understanding of who He is and that salvation can only be received through his son, Jesus Christ. This revelation also demonstrates for us the incredible need for us to go. For some this will become a full-time job, for others, like myself, it will become a launching pad to teaching around the world, which has brought "The Big Four" into clear view for me.

My question is, what will it take to bring into your view the reality of fulfilling the Mathew 28 and Mark 16 mandate?

Lesson for Chapter 7

Disciples and Their World

DISCIPLES ARE COMMITTED TO INFLUENCING THEIR WORLD, BEING OBEDIENT TO THE GREAT COMMANDMENT (MARK 16:15-18) AND THE GREAT COMMISSION (MATT. 28:19-20).

CORE ISSUE: MISSION

1st KEY PASSAGE:

> *Go therefore and make disciples of all nations, baptizing them in the name of the Father and of the Son and of the Holy Spirit, teaching them to observe all that I have commanded you. And behold, I am with you always, to the end of the age. (Matt. 28:19-20)*

2nd KEY PASSAGE:

> *Whoever believes and is baptized will be saved, but whoever does not believe will be condemned. And these signs will accompany those who believe: in my name they will cast out demons; they will speak in new tongues; they will pick up serpents with their hands; and if they drink any deadly poison, it will not hurt them; they will lay their hands on the sick, and they will recover. (Mark 16:16-18)*

BACKGROUND:

A benefit of growing up in one area and staying there most of your life is that you know just about everyone, and everyone seems to know you. Nevertheless, our culture is highly mobile, and many people never even meet their neighbors. We are all different and have varied life experiences. What is someone else's world and life like? The vital element in building relationships is a "Jumping Culture" phenomenon. Today we must ask ourselves to not only look at the back of the head of the person sitting in front of you in a church service, but apply a relationship principle, get to know at least their first name. You may find yourself praying for a fellow believer that is in desperate need.

LET'S READ:

> *For though I am free from all, I have made myself a servant to all, that I might win more of them. To the Jews I became as a Jew, in order to win Jews. To those under the law I became as one under the law (though not being myself under the law) that I might win those under the law. To those outside the law I became as one outside the law (not being outside the law of God but under the law of Christ) that I might win those outside the law. To the weak I became weak, that I might win the weak. I have become all things to all people, that by all means I might save some. I do it all for the sake of the gospel, that I may share with them in its blessings. (1 Cor. 9: 19-23)*

QUESTIONS FOR REFLECTION:

1. What is necessary to connect with people different from us if we hope to have a relationship with them?
2. Why would anyone want to build a bridge with someone beyond cultural or racial barriers? *(See verse 19)*
3. If we could meet Paul, the apostle, and have an unhurried hour with him, what might impress us about him?
4. How would you describe Paul's motivation for making relationships across such a broad spectrum?

CONSIDER THIS:

God is calling you to be a person full of grace and integrity. You know that. However, have you grasped that the Lord is calling you to be a Godly person who, as much as anything, first loves God heartily and completely, and then loves the world of people who need to know Him? To love the world in desperate need means also to make disciples of all nations (all people, all races).

CRITICAL STEPS*

LOVING THE LORD COMPLETELY

1. Sincerely *confess* any sin to the Lord (I John 1:9).
2. *Surrender* to His Lordship in your life (Romans 12:1-2).
3. Set your *affections* on things above (Colossians 3:1-2).

4. Seek to please Him by *obediently* living a life of faith in Him (Hebrews 11:6).

LOVING YOUR NEIGHBORS

1. Love your enemies. Dr. Bill Bright, founder of Campus Crusade for Christ, wrote five vital truths about love.
   a. God loves you unconditionally (Romans 5:8).
   b. You are commanded to love (Mark 12:28-31).
   c. You cannot love in your own strength (John 15:5).
   d. You can love with God's love (Galatians 5:22).
   e. You love by faith (Hebrews 11: 6).
2. Bless others. This means to speak well of others and be friendly to them. Bear no negative report about them.
3. Do good toward others. Find ways to make life easier for them.
4. Pray for them. Praying for others to come to the Lord is what Paul told Timothy to do.

First of all, then, I urge that requests, prayers, intercessions, and thanks be offered on behalf of all people. (1Timothy 2:1)

MAKING DISCIPLES:

1. Be friendly and build a bridge with the other person. Use this contact as an opportunity to confirm their salvation.
2. Make sure they have a Bible and that they are integrated into the life of a local church and a disciple-type small group.

3. Begin to teach biblically what it means to be a person of Christ-like integrity. It is essential at this point to help them know and obey the Word in the power of the Holy Spirit.

**Taken from Breaking Down the Walls—A Model of Reconciliation In An Age Of Racial Strife, by Raleigh Washington and Glen Kehrein. © 1993, Raleigh Washington and Glen Kehrein, Moody Press. (Used by Permission).*

Personal Evaluation *(On Your Own)*

On a scale of 1-10 (1 being "I totally disagree" and 10 being "I totally agree), rate yourself in the following areas:

1. In your mind or on paper, make a list of everyone you don't like or who has hurt you in the past, and you find hard to love. Keep this list private. Now, pray for each person on that list. Can you decide today to love each of them by faith?
2. Make a list of people you know who probably do not know Christ. Will you pray daily for them to be saved?
3. I will faithfully share the Gospel with others.

(In the Group)

1. What are some ways to reach out to non-Christians to show that Jesus completely loves them?
2. How can you build a bridge toward your neighbor to show how much you do love them?
3. How can you turn a secular conversation with an unsaved person into a spiritual conversation and then into a Gospel presentation?

Closing the Gap on Promise Chapter 7

A DISCIPLE IS COMMITTED TO INFLUENCING THEIR WORLD, BEING OBEDIENT TO THE GREAT COMMANDMENT (MARK 12:30-31) AND THE GREAT COMMISSION (MATT. 28:19-20).

Setting A Prayerful Horizon:

Lord willing, six months from now, my life will reflect this promise in these ways:

Accountability Commitment:

By now, you should feel that you can make a commitment to meet regularly with some of your brothers.

Who:______________________________________

When:_____________________________________

**Adapted from Go the Distance, edited by John Trent and published by Focus on the Family, ©1996 by Promise Keepers. All rights reserved. International copyright secured. (Used by permission).*

Chapter 8

What about the Women?

WOMEN AS DISCIPLES ARE COMMITTED TO INFLUENCING THEIR WORLD, BEING OBEDIENT TO THE WORD (ROMANS 16:7) AND TEACHING THE WORD OF GOD (ACTS 18:18)

As the books of Samuel and Kings unfold, they tell of the incredible rise of the nation of Israel through the leadership of David and Solomon. Hannah's son, Samuel, whom she promised to give back to God, became instrumental in the nation's ascent. These glory days of Israel can be traced back to the heart cries of a barren but fully surrendered, godly woman. [23]

(Read: 1 Samuel 1:10-18)

Hannah was a woman experiencing the unspeakable agony of infertility. When Eli questions her unusual prayer style, Hannah says, "I was pouring out my soul to the Lord." Hannah instinctively knew the searing heartbreak that was filling up her soul had to be prayed for! She knew if she did not pray out her

[23] Emerson, Alain; Cox, Adam. The God Story: Encountering Unfailing Love in the Unfolding Narrative of Scripture (pp. 105-107). (Function). Kindle Edition.

sorrow, it would destroy her, so she held nothing back. Hannah pours everything out before the face of her compassionate God. When Eli accused her of being drunk, Hannah cried out to him;

> *"Do not regard your servant as a worthless woman, for all along I have been speaking out of my great anxiety and vexation." Then Eli answered, "Go in peace, and the God of Israel grant your petition that you have made to him." And she said, "Let your servant find favor in your eyes." Then the woman went her way and ate, and her face was no longer sad.*
>
> *They rose early in the morning and worshiped before the Lord; then they went back to their house at Ramah. And Elkanah knew Hannah his wife, and the Lord remembered her. And in due time Hannah conceived and bore a son, and she called his name Samuel, for she said, "I have asked for him from the Lord." (1 Sam. 1:16–20)*

I can see a lot of Hannah's tears in others, and read about where the Bible mentions seven prominent women who would bear sons who would become great leaders in Israel.

Sarah (Genesis 18:10-14): God promised Abraham a son, and Sarah, despite her age, conceived Isaac.

Rebekah (Genesis 25:21): Isaac prayed for his barren wife, and she conceived twins, Esau and Jacob.

Rachel (Genesis 30:1-2): Longing for children, she eventually bore Joseph after God opened her womb.

Hannah (1 Samuel 1-2): She prayed fervently for a son and God granted her Samuel, the great prophet.

Manoah's Wife (Judges 13): An unnamed woman, told by an angel she would bear a son, Samson, the mighty judge.

The Shunammite Woman (2 Kings 4:8-44): A wealthy woman who showed hospitality to Elisha, who prophesied she would have a son.

Elizabeth (Luke 1): She and her husband Zechariah were old and childless until God opened her womb to bear John the Baptist.

These examples remind us that someone's "broken hallelujah" prayers may be transformed into songs of joy. The outpouring of an honest heart can be the receptacle for the dreams of God. All of these women's sons became prominent and instrumental in the history of Israel. When we look at God's timetable, his timing, I think of two words, *Kairos* and *Kronos.* The term *Kronos* is the time we spend living our lives and doing our work. *Kairos* is God's intervention into time at a certain time with a certain purpose and His work at that time.

My mother was 30 years old when she gave birth to me. I don't know if she was barren, but in those days, women were getting married and having children at 15 years of age and so on. That means my birth was late for my mom, who had three C-sections, which was ill-advised in the 1950s. However, this was a Kairos moment for God in my family.

We cannot fail to mention others in addition to these prominent women in the Bible who birthed prominent men. There were several prophets, ministers and leaders who were women in the biblical text.

Deborah (Judges 4-5): The most prominent female leader, a prophetess who judged Israel.

Miriam (Exodus 15:20): A prophetess and leader alongside Moses and Aaron.

Huldah (2 Kings 22:14-20): A prophetess whose inspired words from God led King Josiah.

Anna (Luke 2:36-38): An elderly prophetess in the Temple.

Philip's Daughters (Acts 21:8-9): Four virgin daughters of Philip the Evangelist who prophesied.

My paternal grandmother, Pearl Barber, and my mother, Mella Barber, remind me of these matriarchs. In the Apostle Paul's words to Timothy in his letter in 2 Timothy, he admonishes him to not forget the words of his mother and grandmother. As I process this passage of scripture, I see them applying to me:

I am reminded of your sincere faith, a faith that dwelt first in your grandmother Lois and your mother Eunice and now, I am sure, dwells in you as well. (2 Tim. 1:5)

Most Sundays and Wednesdays, my grandmother Pearl would say, "Come on, Jimmy. We're going to church because you're gonna be a preacher one day!" I loathed those words, and as I shared earlier, I ran from them into the waywardness of "Sex, Drugs and Rock N Roll," the popular saying of the 60s, 70s, and 80s. I told Grandma the preachers were big and fat and sweated, and they spit a lot. If I was sweating, I wanted it to be on the football field like Jim Brown, a famous black football player in the National Football League with the Cleveland Browns (1957-1965).

I became prominent at my alma mater Virginia Tech, holding several records for touchdowns, all-purpose yardage, and pass catches. I played with the Houston Texans in the World Football League until I injured my leg. I gave up professional football and coached running backs for 5 years at my alma mater Virginia Tech.

When I was 30 years old, my mom called me after I had been terminated from the coaching position at Virginia Tech. College and professional football is very volatile as a profession, even in today's game when it comes to holding onto your position as a coach. She reminded me of that call to preach that came from grandma. She had heard from my sister about the terrible lifestyle I was living in the very low, or I would say the lowest places in my life. For some reason, she and my grandmother, Pearl, knew that I was to be a man chasing after God's heart and to teach the Word of God to the Church and to the world.

My philosophy at that time was to run from, and not chase after God. One day, I ran into Him headlong. On October 17, 1982, I heard the Lord Jesus Christ ask me to agree with him, which also meant to follow him. My life has had many drastic 180 degree turning points since that time and continues to do so today. As I travel, as I teach, and as I am completing this writing, I am reminded of the influence, teaching and discipleship of the many men and the many women who have been an influence and direction in my life.

Meeting Dr. Cook

I initially met Dr. Nancy Cook, who was the senior pastor of a little church named Tulsa Christian Center Ministries (TCCM) in Tulsa, Oklahoma. As a student in one of my classes, *Introduction to Pastoral Care,* in the summer of 2008 she was one of those women that I admire, who were getting theologically educated. A woman already called to preach the Word of God, she wanted to hear from the ORU professors to affirm and confirm her calling, as many denominations don't affirm or confirm women as ordained ministers and definitely not as senior pastors. Oral Roberts has had famous women preach on the campus, confirming miracles through women like Marilyn Hickey and Kathryn Kuhlman, not to mention the numerous doctoral professors teaching in the five accredited programs at Oral Robert university.

When I was teaching the class and discussing reaching out into a world that was in desperate need of Jesus Christ, I had attempted to meet many of those needs on mission trips to India, Mexico, Russia, Europe, and Fiji. I would ask every one of the students their degree plan, their course of study, and what they wanted to receive from this class as it relates to their future and ministry. When I asked the questions of the now Dr. Cook, she replied,

> *We don't do much, but we have a small church meeting every Sunday and Wednesday, and we minister twice a month to the men and women at the John 3:16 Mission in downtown Tulsa, and I teach with Reza Safa a podcast that is broadcast into the Middle East.*

I replied that my experience involved more activities than what is typical for an average professor. She responded in class by suggesting, given my world travel and teaching background, *"Dr. Barber, you should come and help us."*

Her request was stated clearly and made an impression on me. I have had many students ask me to help them, but Dr. Cook's request hit me differently. As I considered it, I reflected that since I had experience with jumping culture, shouldn't I help the homeless population in Tulsa do the same? This request from her occasioned three convincing dreams which I know today were from God and initiated by the intercessors of her church who were praying for us to come and help them. From the time in 2008 that Dr. Cook and the intercessors from her church prayed, Addie and I have been in the ministry with Dr. Cook.

When I began doing ministry work at TCCM, it was not only a request from her, but one from the Holy Spirit of God that opened up a new avenue for me to be a voice and an advocate for women to be heard.

What About the Women

It is here that I want to discuss women in leadership in the New Testament Church. A lot of the controversy about women leading comes from the passages in 1 Corinthians 11, and 1 Corinthians 14. Many have taken these passages out of context in relation to each other by saying that women should be silent in the church.

> *1 Corinthians 11:5. woman . . . prayeth . . . prophesieth — This instance of women speaking in public worship is an extraordinary case and justified only by the miraculous gifts which such women possessed as their credentials; for instance, Anna the prophetess and Priscilla (so Acts 2:18). The ordinary rule to them is: silence in public (1 Corinthians 14:34, 35; 1 Timothy 2:11, 12). Mental receptivity and activity in family life are recognized in Christianity, as most accordant with the destiny of woman. This passage does not necessarily sanction women speaking in public, even though possessing miraculous gifts; but simply records what took place at Corinth, without expressing an opinion on it, reserving the censure of it till 1 Corinthians 14:34, 35. Even those women endowed with prophecy were designed to exercise their gift, rather in other times and places, than the public congregation.*[24]

Women preached and prophesied throughout the biblical text. The controversy in Corinth was typical of the culture. When we take culture and scripture out of context, we literally hamstring the church. As a result, we have put the church behind several decades, which is sadly common throughout the history and theology of the church. It's not that women want leadership or beg for it. I believe it comes as part of a calling on their lives to fulfill the mandate for the last day's Call of God.

One day, Dr. Cook asked me if we could both teach during the summer months. She suggested that we could each teach lessons related to our thesis topics. My thesis was on

[24] Robert Jamieson, A. R. Fausset, and David Brown, *A Commentary, Critical and Explanatory on the Whole Bible*, 1871, Accordance electronic ed. (Altamonte Springs: OakTree Software, 1996), paragraph 21307.

"Discipleship," while her thesis topic was on "Forgiveness." I was ecstatic to associate with Dr. Cook as a female senior pastor and her work at TCCM, and its association with the John 3:16 Mission to the homeless and marginalized in Tulsa, Oklahoma.

The John 3:16 Mission Director and President Steve Whitaker invited Dr. Cook to come and teach in the chapel services conducted there because of the influx of the homeless women coming into the homeless shelter. Whitaker had suggested they needed a woman's presence, and he believed Dr. Cook had the credentials from a major university, OSU and ORU, with certified counseling skills, and the teaching ability to satisfy a tremendous gap in the church and seminaries around the country.

Mind you that President Whitaker was a Baptist minister, and that Baptist theology opposed women being ministers in the church, let alone Spirit-empowered women. I applaud President Whitaker for "Jumping Culture" to that which has been taught and lived out for centuries.

One day, as we were preparing to teach the summer classes, I was approached by one of the ladies of the church, Lu Arnold, who asked the question, *"Dr. Barber, I know that your thesis was about men, but what about the women?"*

This did not startle me, because Lu was a strong leader and intercessor at TCCM. She was one of the first women that encouraged me about the viability and the safe haven for the men and women in the John 3:16 Mission. She would meet me at the Mission and show me how this group of homeless individuals were so much a part of the society and the church.

Initially, years earlier, I had planned to include both women and men in my thesis project in the Single Adult Ministry, however, that scope was too broad for a D.Min. Thesis project. I was advised to focus solely on men's discipleship in small groups. Lu's request then required me to revise my workbook wording to include women, as the group composition had changed.

During my initial visit to Fiji, I encountered an intriguing question from Pastor Mary, the wife of Pastor Suliasi Kurulo, Senior Pastor of Christian Ministry Fellowship International (CMFI). Based at the World Harvest Centre, Suva, Fiji, CMFI is a church ministry. While conducting a class on pastoral care, she inquired, "Dr. Barber, what about the women?" This solidified the inclusion of this chapter to "Come Follow Me."

What Does The Text Say

The Bible shows that both the Old and New Testaments valued women and included them in discipleship. Jesus' ministry promoted women and men, challenging social norms across both Testaments. The former Associate Dean at the ORU-STM, Dr. Cheryl Iverson, shared a teaching on the female presence in the biblical text starting with the Proverbs 31 woman and other women in ministry.

> *Strength and dignity are her clothing, and she laughs at the time to come. She opens her mouth with wisdom, and the teaching of kindness is on her tongue. She looks good at the ways of her household and does not eat the bread of idleness. Her children (students) rise up and call her blessed; her husband also praises her. Many women have done excellently, but you surpass them all. (Prov 31:25-29)*

Female Prophets and Ministers

Dr. Iverson reiterates that Apostle Paul had women on his ministry team. The Bible clearly records the names of the women who served as deacons, pastors, prophets, and apostles in the New Testament church.

They include Priscilla, Phoebe, Euodia, Syntyche, Nympha, Traephena, Traephosa, Philip's four daughters, and Junia (see Rom. 16:7)—a female apostle who spent time in prison with Paul. (Her Roman name was always listed in early biblical manuscripts as feminine until the 13th century when some translators decided a woman couldn't possibly be a church planter.) Iverson continues,

> *It is without a doubt that women had a contributing part in the biblical text supporting what the church has become today. The planting of the church and participation as disciples that followed Jesus Christ and other patriarchs in the biblical text is evident.*

She continues an expose of many of the encounters of women that were involved or followed Jesus throughout the biblical narrative.

Women accompanied Jesus

> *Soon afterward he went on through cities and villages, proclaiming and bringing the good news of the kingdom of God. And the twelve were with him, and also some women who had been healed of evil spirits and infirmities: Mary, called Magdalene, from whom seven demons had gone out,*

and Joanna, the wife of Chuza, Herod's household manager, and Susanna, and many others, who provided for them out of their means. (Luke 8:1–3)

Mary at the Feet of Jesus

Mary, who sat at the feet of Jesus, exemplifies women being disciples. Martha expressed her frustration to Jesus, stating that she needed Mary's assistance. While Martha attended to her duties in the kitchen, Mary remained at Jesus' feet, listening attentively.

And she had a sister called Mary, who sat at the Lord's feet and listened to his teaching." (Luke 10:39). Mary which also — "who for her part," in contrast with Martha. sat — "seated herself." From the custom of sitting beneath an instructor, the phrase "sitting at one's feet" came to mean being a disciple of someone (Acts 22:3). heard — rather, "kept listening" to His word.[25]

The Samaritan at the Well

A woman from Samaria came to draw water. Jesus said to her, "Give me a drink." (For his disciples had gone away into the city to buy food.) The Samaritan woman said to him, "How is it that you, a Jew, ask for a drink from me, a woman of Samaria?" (For Jews have no dealings with Samaritans.) Jesus answered her, "If you knew the gift of God, and who it is that is saying to you, 'Give me a drink,'

[25] Robert Jamieson, A. R. Fausset, and David Brown, *A Commentary, Critical and Explanatory on the Whole Bible*, 1871, Accordance electronic ed. (Altamonte Springs: OakTree Software, 1996), paragraph 18249.

you would have asked him, and he would have given you living water. (John 4:7–10).

The text narrative above is a conversation between the Samaritan women at the well originally dug in the town of Samaria called Sychar, near the field that Jacob had given to his son Joseph. The narrative shows that Jesus came to this region to share his message to the Samaritan people whose roots have a Jewish ethos (John 4:5-46).

So, we see that Jesus chose the route on purpose, knowing there were two possible routes from Judea to Galilee. The longer route was through Gentile country on the east side of the Jordan; the shorter was through Samaria and was most used in spite of the animosity between the Jews and the Samaritans. Verse 4 suggests this latter route was chosen as an obligation to and for Samaria. Perhaps John is implying that there was divine reason as far as Jesus was concerned.

Two Jewish prejudices—conversation with a Samaritan and conversation with a woman were overcome by Jesus' actions.[26]

The Widow Seeking Justice

And he told them a parable to the effect that they ought always to pray and not lose heart. He said, "In a certain city there was a judge who neither feared God nor respected man. And there was a widow in that city who kept coming to him and saying, 'Give me justice against my adversary.' For a while he refused, but afterward he said to himself,

[26] Donald Guthrie, *John*, ed. D. A Carson et al., New Bible Commentary: 21st Century Edition. Accordance electronic ed. (Downers Grove: InterVarsity Press, 1994), 1032.

'Though I neither fear God nor respect man, yet because this widow keeps bothering me, I will give her justice, so that she will not beat me down by her continual coming.' (Luke 18:1-5)

The Poor Widow Giving Her Offering.

Jesus looked up and saw the rich putting their gifts into the offering box, and he saw a poor widow put in two small copper coins. And he said, 'Truly, I tell you, this poor widow has put in more than all of them. For they all contributed out of their abundance, but she in her poverty put in all she had to live on'. (Luke 21:1–4)

Daughter of Abraham

Then the Lord answered him, 'You hypocrites! Does not each of you on the Sabbath untie his ox or his donkey from the manger and lead it away to water it? And ought not this woman, a daughter of Abraham whom Satan bound for eighteen years, be loosed from this bond on the Sabbath day?' As he said these things, all his adversaries were put to shame, and all the people rejoiced at all the glorious things that were done by him. (Luke 13:15–17)

Brother, Sister, And Mother

While he was still speaking to the people, behold, his mother and his brothers stood outside, asking to speak to him. But he replied to the man who told him, 'Who is my mother, and who are my brothers?' And stretching out his hand toward his disciples, he said, 'Here are my mother and my brothers! For whoever does the will of my Father in heaven is my brother and sister and mother.' (Matthew 12:46–50).

Taught Theology As Disciples'

Now as they went on their way, Jesus entered a village. And a woman named Martha welcomed him into her house. And she had a sister called Mary, who sat at the Lord's feet and listened to his teaching. But Martha was distracted with much serving. And she went up to him and said, 'Lord, do you not care that my sister has left me to serve alone? Tell her then to help me.' But the Lord answered her, 'Martha, Martha, you are anxious and troubled about many things, but one thing is necessary. Mary has chosen the good portion, which will not be taken away from her.' (Luke 10:38–42).

First To Witness The Resurrection

And behold, Jesus met them and said, "Greetings!" And they came up and took hold of his feet and worshiped him. Then Jesus said to them, 'Do not be afraid; go and tell my brothers to go to Galilee, and there they will see me.' (Matt. 28:9-10)

Dr. Iverson concludes that as we have observed, the life of Jesus had women as disciples, as can be seen if one were to peruse the text related to the occasions when He was with them. Most of the time we don't see them being called disciples, but you don't always hear of the only followers of Jesus being just men either.

As I have previously quoted from Dr. Charles Snow, "A disciple is a loyal learning follower of Jesus Christ." In that regard I propose another look at the biblical text from a theological, exegetical, and hermeneutical aspect. For too long have we rejected women based on simple psychological and eisegetical interpretation, i.e., reading one's own ideas or biases into the text rather than understanding true exegesis, which is understanding the original meaning intended by the author. This contrast to the two types of interpretation, sometimes fails to draw out a true meaning of the intent of the author. It's also known as "reading into the text," i.e., changing the Word of God to mean what some people want it to mean. It is time to turn it around and "Jump Culture" for Christ's sake to interpret the true meaning of God's intention for women.

Lesson for Chapter 8

What about the women?

The text many times says that people followed him and listened to his teaching, and many believed. As we look at the text again in the book of Luke chapter 8, we see the names of women disciples. I might add that I believe that there were more. These were the more prominent ones mentioned in the text that followed Jesus.

> *Soon afterward he went on through cities and villages, proclaiming and bringing the good news of the kingdom of God. And the twelve were with him, and also some women who had been healed of evil spirits and infirmities: Mary, called Magdalene, from whom seven demons had gone out, and Joanna, the wife of Chuza, Herod's household manager, and Susanna, and many others, who provided for them out of their means. (Luke 8:1–3)*

Luke mentions a number of women, as we see here, who took part in Jesus' work and helped to provide for the needs of himself, and the group which included his male companions. This story illustrates the accusation that was made in Lk 7:34. Jesus had been invited to the home of a Pharisee, called Simon, probably for a meal after a synagogue service. It was not uncommon for uninvited guests to be found at a banquet, and among them was a woman well-known as a prostitute.

I. Howard Marshall, in the *New Bible Commentary: 21st Century Edition* makes mention that since people reclined on couches instead of sitting on chairs to eat formal meals, this lady was easily able to reach Jesus. She proceeded to anoint Jesus with perfume, very possibly bought with her immoral earnings, but she could not finish her task for tears. Her actions were no doubt unseemly, but she was under too great emotional stress to care what people thought.

The Pharisee was disturbed by the way in which Jesus accepted this respect given by such an undesirable person in so embarrassing a manner. His feeling that Jesus might be a prophet was contradicted by Jesus' being seemingly unaware that the person touching him was a sinner—and therefore "unclean."

But Jesus knew what was happening and made his point to Simon with a parable whose message was quite clear: love is the proof that a person has received forgiveness, and the more people are forgiven, the more they will love.

Some commentaries have argued that the woman's love for Jesus was the *cause* of her forgiveness rather than its result.

> *They would interpret (Lk.7:47) to mean: 'the reason her sins are forgiven is that she loved much' and then see (v. 48) as the first declaration of forgiveness to her. This view would make nonsense of the parable (vv. 41-42), which clearly teaches that love follows forgiveness, and it ignores the stress on faith in (v. 50). The error is due to not recognizing that "to love" is the Hebrew phrase for "to show gratitude". We*

must assume that the woman had previously heard and accepted the gospel message.[27]

Reflection:

Women are always seeking God for a change, especially a change in or for other people for whom they care. I find this to be an amazing strength of women. They pray at a higher level and with deeper care, conviction, and concern than most men. That is a concern I believe reaches the heart of God like no other prayer. For women who seek God's face not only for themselves but for the men, women, and children that they birth, care about, and love. It seems to be their prayers that succeed and reach God more than the prayers of others and other types of prayer. I do not mean categories; I mean it is the *depth of their prayer* in whatever category, i.e., corporate, intercession, personal, work, etc. For women who are desperate, their prayers reach God's Spirit more, as I have seen in the prayers of my grandmother, my mother, Pastor Sue Farrar, and my wife, Adeline.

My wife recently had a dream where she saw the cloud of witnesses that included these women above, interceding specifically for the success of my life and ministry. God knows where we are and what he has to do to get us where he wants us to be, and that very often will include the ministry and intercession of women. Amen!

---

[27] I. Howard Marshall, *New Bible Commentary: 21st Century Edition* (Downers Grove: InterVarsity Press, 1994), Accordance electronic ed., 992.

Questions for reflection.

1. Who were the individuals, especially women, that mentored and prayed for you?
2. What are some prayers, if you can recall, that were prayed by women over you that are coming to pass now?
3. When we look at other women e.g., mothers, teachers, which ones, if you can recall, encouraged you to get to where you are today?
4. When looking at the story of Samuel's mother, and the women in my story, do you think God listens to the prayers of a mother or woman more than the prayers of most men? Why or why not?
5. After reading this lesson what new avenues of change will you implement or discuss with men and/or women relative to women in Ministry?

Prayer:

Father, help me to live this day in my life to full ability being true to You, in every way. Help me not to neglect, in even the slightest way people from other cultures and especially women. Jesus, help me to give myself away to others that you might lead me to, and help me also to be kind to everyone I meet. Spirit, help me to love the lost, proclaiming Christ in all I do and say, Amen!

CONCLUSION

THE REWARD OF BEING A DISCIPLE

As I finish this work, I remember how it started. In 1975, when I called Dr. LeRoy Eims, author of *The Lost Art of Discipleship,* to get permission to use his book for my thesis, he asked if I was reviving his philosophy. I excitedly said yes, as it aligns with the biblical mandate from Jesus in Matthew 28: 16-20, "The Great Commission."

This commission has not ceased since that time, and the journey has brought significant rewards. As Dr. Snow describes, "A disciple is a loyal, learning follower of Jesus Christ." My journey towards discipleship began early in my life, influenced primarily by my parents James Sr. and Mella Barber and my grandmother, Pearl Barber. However, during the summer, my mother preferred that we attend vacation Bible school at the Baptist Church. The Baptist Church was vibrant with music and highly focused on ensuring individuals received Jesus as their Lord and Savior. While it appeared they assumed attendees of the vacation Bible school were saved, I recall being asked collectively, rather than individually, if I knew Jesus Christ as my Lord and Savior. In contrast, as Presbyterians, we believed salvation was assured by attending church every Sunday.

Whether you were neglected or totally cared for, we have all been indoctrinated, taught, and nurtured with an influence of the two greatest aspects of life, namely, the dichotomy of hatred versus love. These two forces have existed since Satan waged war in Heaven and will continue throughout this season until the end of all things, when God will establish a new heaven and a new earth. We will stand before the Judgement Seat for those who find Jesus Christ as Lord, or the Great White Throne for those who join in the war against God, His Son Jesus Christ and the Holy Spirit.

The choice to become or reject becoming a believer in Jesus Christ is inevitable, we all will make one choice or the other. I pray that it will happen for most people before passing into eternity from this earth that you make Jesus Christ Lord and "Enter In" and receive your reward at the judgment seat of Christ.

As a hospice chaplain, I have seen people reject the call to be a believer and negate heaven. I personally think God wants to re-populate the heavens, essentially, with that number of angels that fell with Satan. I think that is what the text means when the Apostle Paul discusses the fullness of the Gentiles in Romans 11:25-27.

> *Lest you be wise in your own sight, I do not want you to be unaware of this mystery, brothers: a partial hardening has come upon Israel, until the fullness of the Gentiles has come in. And in this way all Israel will be saved, as it is*

written, 'The Deliverer will come from Zion, he will banish ungodliness from Jacob, and this will be my covenant with them when I take away their sins.' (Rom. 11:25-27)

My New Testament Theology teacher, Dr. Trevor Grizzle, recapitulates that God sees culture in the context of Romans 11, and culture either accepts or negates God's plan in their lives. Douglas Moo, in The Bible Commentary, states:

'All Israel will be saved'. The hope for a new restoration of Israel that Paul has hinted at throughout verses 11–24 now asserted in the form of a revelation of a it mystery. Paul's use of this term is based on the Old Testament (Dan. 2:2-730,4;4:9) and Jewish Apocalyptic conception to which God's plan for history is fully determined but hidden and awaiting its revelation at the proper moment. See (1 Cor. 2:7; Eph. 3:9; Col. 1:26-27). A primary component of this now revealed mystery for Paul is the way in which God is now working with the gentiles. It is not surprising that Paul labels the oscillation between Jews and gentiles and God's plan for salvation a 'mystery.' Verse 25 in summary restates the process that Paul has sketched several times, 'Israel has experienced a hardening in part until the full number of gentiles has come in.' God's hardening of Jews as Paul has shown in verses 3-10 is partial, for some Jews are coming to Christ and being saved. He has more than once hinted at the temporal limitation of this hardening, which he now makes explicit: it will last only until the divinely determined number of gentiles has come into the kingdom of God (cf. also Luke 21:24).[28]

[28] Douglas J. Moo, *Romans*, ed. D. A Carson et al., New Bible Commentary: 21st Century Edition. Accordance electronic ed. (Downers Grove: InterVarsity Press, 1994), 1148.

In Genesis Chapter 11, at the tower of Babel, Dr. Grizzle iterates that mankind is rejected. In the rejection, God confuses and confounds their languages. Grizzle says that there is a Reversal of that rejection in Acts Chapter 2. On the day of Pentecost, men (of Israel) who were now from every nation and tongue understood everybody in their own language, which Grizzle maintains is a miracle of speaking and of hearing.

God has a purpose that we need to understand, beginning in Genesis 11:1-9, which we can look at in the negative light because God confounded the languages of all men and women. Then He reverses it in Acts 2:1-42, and finally, it all culminates in Revelation 7:9-17. These three chapters point to the work of God. I believe it will be achieved through the work of the Holy Spirit, intervening in the activity of men and women, and the work He wishes to perform. It is very profound, and I encourage you to read all three of the mentioned passages and begin to see the connection of what has been planned from the beginning of time.

Three signals announced to the world that the Holy Spirit had arrived in a new and spectacular way. The plan of God would come through sound, sight, and speech. The *sound* was the first signal of the Spirit's coming. Luke said it was "a sound like the blowing of a violent wind" (2:2). The Spirit's coming at Pentecost disclosed a spectacular *sight*. The disciples "saw what seemed to be tongues of fire" (v. 3). It provoked amazement and wonder. The *speech* was the third sign of the Spirit. The disciples experienced something that was inwardly transforming. Through the impetus of the Spirit, they spoke in languages they had never learned.

The audible, visible, and verbal were outward and inward experiences. Together, they made an overwhelming impact. They provided incontestable proof that the believers were filled with the Holy Spirit. The Spirit-filled person is saturated with divine life and controlled by the Holy Spirit.

> *If wind and fire recall the giving of the Law at Sinai, tongues remind us of Babel (Genesis 11:1-9). At Babel, human arrogance led to the confusion of language and the dispersion of the nations. At Pentecost, human surrender re-established communication and community. Pentecost is Babel reversed. There, confusion of languages ceased, and a new fusion began.*[29]

I believe a greater work of the Holy Spirit finally comes in (Rev. 7:9-17). Please read these passages of the culmination of this great sight, sound, and speech phenomenon. What God has ordained will come to pass. It is basically the process of discipleship culminating from a revival and a harvest of all believers being as one group of "loyal, learning, followers of Jesus Christ!"

I recently resigned from my position at ORU as the Director of the Doctor of Ministry program. It was during the time for renewal of our annual contracts when I had a dream, where ultimately Jesus told me, "*Go finish what I told you to do!*" In the dream, I was taken to, I believe, the place that I can only describe as the holding place in hell. At the time, I did not know where I was, but I was floating along in a cavern with what I can only describe as an angel. I have come to understand

[29] Trevor Grizzle, *Church Aflame: An Exposition of Acts 1-12.* Kindle Edition 603 of 4019, 25.

that this was nothing less than an epiphany of Jesus Christ. We came to a place that I thought was a large body of white water, but I realized there were giant worms writhing over each other. Behind me, I felt the heat of what I knew was a lake of fire. Suddenly, I heard a voice that said, "This is where the worm does not die, and the fire is not quenched." From two passages I was familiar with:

> *And they shall go out and look on the dead bodies of the men who have rebelled against me. For their worm shall not die, their fire shall not be quenched, and they shall be an abhorrence to all flesh. (Is. 66:24).*

> *Where their worm does not die and the fire is not quenched. (Mark 9:48)*

Suddenly, I realized I was in hell. The angel then pointed to my left at a door that was open and a stairway leading upward. I heard the angel of the Lord say, *"Go and finish what I called you to do."* I knew immediately that was the original reason that Addie and I had to come to Oral Roberts University. Under the care and financial contribution of our Pastor, Dr. Larry Lea, with teaching and ministry prep from COTR and ORU, we were to prepare to go into the world and make disciples of all nations, as it had been prophesied.

I believe that we are in the final episodes of the last days of the quest that God has been planning for over 2000 years. On the Jewish calendar it's almost 6000 years since God called mankind back to himself. I believe his calling is the same for most of us, to facilitate the realization of his plan. For you to go into all the world, around you, near you, your neighborhood, your city, your state, and your nation and other countries around this globe as the Spirit of God directs.

> *Go therefore and make disciples of all nations, baptizing them in the name of the Father and of the Son and of the Holy Spirit, teaching them to observe all that I have commanded you. And behold, I am with you always, to the end of the age. (Matt. 28:19-20)*

BIBLIOGRAPHY

BOOKS

Bruce, A. B. *The Training of the Twelve*. Grand Rapids: Kregel, 1971.

Carson, D. A., et al. *New Bible Commentary: 21st Century Edition*. Accordance electronic ed. Downers Grove: InterVarsity Press, 1994.

Coleman, Robert E. *The Master Plan of Evangelism*. Old Tappan: Revell, 1964.

Eims, Leroy. *The Lost Art of Disciple Making*. Grand Rapids: Zondervan, 1978.

Grizzle, Trevor. *Church Aflame: An Exposition of Acts 1-12.* Pathway Press, 2000.

Horner, Bob, Ron Ralston, and David Sundae. *Promise Builders: Applying the Seven Promises*. Promise Keepers. Focus on the Family, 1996.

Jamieson, Robert, A. R. Fausset, and David Brown, *A Commentary, Critical and Explanatory on the Whole Bible*. 1871. Accordance electronic ed. Altamonte Springs: OakTree Software, 1996.

Janssen, Al & Larry K. Weeden, ed. *Seven Promises of a Promise Keeper*: Promise Keepers. Focus on the Family, 1994.

Lea, Larry. *Could You Not Tarry: Learning the Joy of Prayer.* Altamonte Springs, FL Creation House. 1987.

Lehane, by Dennis. *Gone Baby Gone.* William Morrow & Co. 1998.

Marshall, I. Howard. "The woman who was a sinner." *New Bible Commentary: 21st Century Edition.* Downers Grove: InterVarsity Press, 1994.

Moo, Douglas J. "Romans." *New Bible Commentary: 21st Century Edition* (Downers Grove: InterVarsity Press, 1994)

Stedman, Ray *Body Life.* Glendale: Regal, 1972.

Trent, John, ed. *Go the Distance.* Promise Keepers. Focus on the Family, 1996.

Weatherhead, Leslie *Discipleship.* London: SCM Press, 1958.

MISCELLANEOUS

The Navigators, *Design for Discipleship.* Colorado Springs: NavPress, 1973.

"*Gone Baby Gone*" A 2007 movie directed by Ben Affleck. Screenplay by Ben Affleck and Aaron Stockard. Based on the book *Gone Baby Gone* by Dennis Lehane. William Morrow & Co., 1998.

Bible Books Abbreviations

Old Testament

Genesis: Gen.
Exodus: Exod.
Leviticus: Lev.
Numbers: Num.
Deuteronomy: Deut.
Joshua: Josh.
Judges: Judg.
Ruth: Ruth
1 Samuel: 1 Sam.
2 Samuel: 2 Sam.
1 Kings: 1 Kgs.
2 Kings: 2 Kgs.
1 Chronicles: 1 Chr.
2 Chronicles: 2 Chr.
Ezra: Ezra
Nehemiah: Neh.
Esther: Esth.
Job: Job
Psalms: Ps.
Proverbs: Prov.
Ecclesiastes: Eccl.
Song of Solomon: Song
Isaiah: Isa.
Jeremiah: Jer.
Lamentation: Lam.
Ezekiel: Ezek.
Daniel: Dan.
Hosea: Hos.
Joel: Joel
Amos: Amos
Obadiah: Obad.
Jonah: Jonah
Micah: Mic.
Nahum: Nah.
Habakkuk: Hab.
Zephaniah: Zeph.
Haggai: Hag.
Zechariah: Zech.
Malachi: Mal.

New Testament

Matthew: Matt.
Mark: Mark
Luke: Luke
John: John
Acts: Acts
Romans: Rom.
1 Corinthians: 1 Cor.
2 Corinthians: 2 Cor.
Galatians: Gal.
Ephesians: Eph.
Philippians: Phil.
Colossians: Col.

1 Thessalonians: 1 Thess.
2 Thessalonians: 2 Thess.
1 Timothy: 1 Tim.
2 Timothy: 2 Tim.
Titus: Titus
Philemon: Phlm.
Hebrews: Heb.
James: Jas.
1 Peter: 1 Pet.
2 Peter: 2 Pet.
1 John: 1 John
2 John: 2 John
3 John: 3 John
Jude: Jude
Revelation: Rev.

ABOUT THE AUTHOR

Dr. James Barber is the former Director of the Doctor of Ministry (D.Min.) program at Oral Roberts University School of Theology and Ministry (ORU-STM). He continues at ORU as an Adjunct Professor in the ORU Bible Institute. (ORU-BI).

Dr. Barber has taught in the United States, Mexico, Russia, Great Britain, India, and the Fiji Islands. His future objective is to continue teaching both locally and internationally in response to the mandates outlined in Mark 16 and Matthew 28, preparing the next generation of believers. He has been equipped to disciple and prepare future ministers and leaders as mentioned by ORU's founder Dr. Oral Roberts who's mandate and vision continues:

> *"Raise up your students to hear My voice, to go where My light is dim, where My voice is heard small, and My healing power is not known, even to the uttermost bounds of the earth. Their work will exceed yours, and in this I am well pleased.*

He is a carrier and teacher of the Holy Spirit's Gifts as mentioned in the biblical text;

Romans 12:3-8 Motivation Gifts, 1 Corinthians 12:1-11 Manifestation Gifts and Ephesians 4:10 - 14 Management Gifts

Education:

Oral Roberts University. Tulsa, OK. (D.Min.) 1997

Oral Roberts University. Tulsa, OK. (M.Div.) 1991

Virginia Polytechnic Institute & S.U. Blacksburg, VA. (B.S.) 1974

Writing:

Discipling Men through Small Groups in a Local Church. (D.Min. Thesis 1997).

Come Follow Me – Discipleship for the Next Gen (2026)

Ministry & Board Involvement:

- J. Barber Ministries Inc.: Founder & President, 2005 – Present.
- The Pastoral-Care Advisory Group (PAG) at Hillcrest Hospital: Board Member, 2001- Present.
- The Pastoral-Care Advisory Group (PAG) at Jack C. Montgomery VA Hospital: Board Member, 2008- Present.
- World Ministry Fellowship; Plano, TX.; License & Ordained Teacher, Advisory Board member, Ministerial Credentials Committee (MCC): 2008 – Present.
- John 3:16 Mission; Tulsa OK.; Board Member 2015 – 2024.
- Crossroads Hospice Charitable Foundation: Tulsa, OK.; Board Member 2010 –2019.

www.ingramcontent.com/pod-product-compliance
Lightning Source LLC
LaVergne TN
LVHW010100110826
845155LV00028B/424

* 9 7 8 1 9 4 0 9 3 1 2 8 9 *